Teaching after school

Teaching after school

Graeme Kent

Ward Lock Educational

ISBN 0 7062 3052 3

Set in 12 point Monotype Bembo
Printed by Cox & Wyman Limited
London, Fakenham & Reading
for Ward Lock Educational Limited
116 Baker Street, London WIM 2BB
Made in England

Contents

Introduction

Few teachers will pass through their careers without engaging in a variety of extramural activities and few would want to. Despite the occasional comments of the uninformed, teaching is far from being a nine to four profession. Admittedly there are schools at which unwary children daily run the risk of being trampled underfoot in the home-ward bound rush of the staff, but these are rare. Far more common are those schools whose teachers spend much of their spare time in guiding and sharing the interests of the children in their charge. Such teachers do not believe that the life of the school ends with the final bell in the afternoon. Most of them feel that their knowledge of the children may be extended by the close and informal contact which comes with taking an interest in the various out of school games and hobbies. They are convinced that by developing worthwhile recreational interests in each child they are helping to develop the whole child.

The personality of a school is formed in many ways, but chiefly through the efforts of the staff and students working together both in and out of the classroom. Not the least important contribution to this personality comes from those spare time activities in which staff and students mingle freely, sharing ideas and learning from one another.

Assisting with extracurricular activities is not always easy. It can be costly in terms of time and energy expended but such contact between teachers and taught is both rewarding and important and there will always be teachers ready and willing to spend their time freely in such a cause.

What sometimes daunts teachers however is the sheer scope and variety of out of school activities which can range from sophisticated debating and philosophical societies to turning over the soil on the bare patch of earth called the school garden. At various levels teachers may be called upon to take an interest in Scouting, the Red Cross, societies ranging from archaeological to zoological, nature rambles, the Duke of Edinburgh's Award Scheme, helping with closed circuit television programmes, making films and hundreds of other activities.

It is to these teachers that this book is offered, in the hope that some of its hints and suggestions may be of help to them in the wide and almost unlimited field of out of school activities. To all those colleagues who have refereed football matches in the monsoon season, retained their sanity whilst producing the school play, and experienced the ghastly moment of truth which comes with the realization that at least two children in the expedition have been left behind on the station platform, this book is humbly dedicated.

I

Libraries

Libraries in schools can vary from well equipped, sophisticated rooms devoted to the sole purpose of bringing books and children together to a handful of tattered volumes languishing in a classroom corner. The only thing that such diverse organizations will probably have in common is the fact that both are looked after by teachers as an out of school activity.

At the moment few colleges of education or similar institutions provide courses of instruction for the would be teacher librarian, so that the majority of teachers entrusted with the responsibility of looking after a school library have to find their way mainly by a process of trial and error. There are however a number of books on the market which are both useful and practical and these are listed at the end of the chapter.

The need for school libraries

Few teachers would deny the need for school libraries. Books should form an essential part of the education and general background of every child. As Sybil Marshall writes in the March 1968 edition of *School Librarian*:

> What it all adds up to is that we are bound absolutely by two limits. We are bound by time, of which we know we have only such a little bit, and we are bound by our physical roots being in one place . . . . One life is not enough . . . so we turn to the one thing that counts, that gives us more space and more time, and that is the book.

A certain amount of time will be given to reading in the class at all age levels, but the time available for this is necessarily limited and by far the most important aspect of children's reading is that which is done voluntarily in their own time. The services of a good library are needed to encourage the habit of reading and to make a wide selection of books readily available to boys and girls.

In the school library children often make their first contact with a really wide range of well chosen books. Lionel McColvin makes this point in *Libraries for Children* when he says:

Books are means by which man may expand his personal universe, by which he can discover what other people have experienced, thought and discovered; by which he can enjoy unlimited travel in time and space to worlds beyond his own personal ken; and by which he can save himself an immense amount of time and energy by not trying himself to think, do and discover again what other people have thought, done and discovered already.[1]

The school library if it is properly organized should have many uses. It can be a centre for topic and project work, a meeting place, a room in which children can sit and work not only with books but with maps, globes, magazines and pictures as well. It should be a place where they can look for the answers to questions, satisfy established interests and develop new ones.

The physical organization

The actual layout of the library will obviously be determined to a large extent by the space available in a given school and this can vary considerably. Needless to say, a school which can set aside a room or a number of rooms to be used entirely as a library has a considerable advantage over one which has to improvise. All the same a little ingenuity can often work wonders. There is usually a room or a corner somewhere which can be pressed into service to hold the books and other apparatus, although it is better not to use one which is in constant demand as a classroom or is liable to be locked or in any other way inaccessible for long periods.

If no room at all can be found teachers might like to consider storing the books along a well lit corridor, making sure that there is enough space to allow people to pass by and that browsers do not block the passage entirely or in any way contravene school fire regulations.

Care should be taken to ensure that the library is as attractive and comfortable as possible. It should be a place that children look forward to visiting. It is true that not all boys and girls possess a highly developed aesthetic sense and that some share the attitude of the pupil quoted in the Newsom Report when he declared that even if it were made of marble it would still be bloody school, but that is no reason for giving children shoddy surroundings when they can be made pleasant. The contents of the library room will obviously depend upon the amount of money available for furnishing it but even in the barest rooms the floors can be swept, the shelves dusted and lined with clean paper, books bound in plastic covers in order to preserve them and so on.

The shelves on which the books are kept should be no more than

180 mm deep and must be easily accessible. In senior schools the tops of the shelves should be no more than 2·2 m from the ground which means that the books on the top shelves will be only a little over 2 m from the ground. In junior schools the shelves should be lower. If adjustable shelves can be purchased these will be found to be very useful.

Normally the shelves will run round the walls of the library. Sometimes it is possible to have shelves coming out at right angles from the wall as well. These shelves form small alcoves in which private work is possible, although to remove the temptation to procrastinate or make mischief it is usually better to situate the librarian's table so that the librarian can look into the alcoves.

In order to get an idea of the range of library furnishings and accessories available the teacher should send for the catalogues of the various suppliers. I have always found the materials provided by such firms as the Educational Supply Association, Philip and Tacey and James Galt to be of a uniformly high standard, but a number of firms advertise in the educational press and their handbooks will give the teacher an idea of the sheer variety of supplementary material to be found.

Among the fittings and furnishings which will help to make a library easy to run and pleasant to work in are wire bookracks. These can be supplied with stands or may be mounted on walls and enable books to be displayed so that the front cover is on view, or opened at a certain page if topic work or an exhibition is under way.

In a permanent library building the shelves housing the books will be attached to the walls of the room in some way as a rule, but in a temporary library or in an exceptionally large permanent library portable bookcases are recommended. These may be moved at will and can be a considerable help if redistribution of space becomes necessary although it is wise to avoid making islands in the middle of the room as the occasional malcontent or idler tends to lurk behind them in splendid isolation. Wall bookcases can also be purchased and suspended from the wall; these come in units and can be added to when required.

A book trolley for moving books from one part of the library to another will prove very useful and so will book troughs for displaying new books etc.

Another useful addition to a well equipped library are horizontal rails which can be fixed to walls with little trouble and taken down when no longer needed. From these rails vertical units with hinge attachments on which to hang paperback and similar lightweight books can be suspended.

Framed display boards are useful for displays and exhibitions in the library and a large notice board is essential. Pegboard letters and numbers in coloured plastic can be used with pegboards if needed, and a large number of pegboard fittings – flowerpot rings, brackets, bottle stands etc – will all prove useful.

Among the smaller aids for the librarian, all of which may be obtained from the appropriate suppliers, are reference card holders, tickets, date stamps, bookracks, small display easels, endorsing ink and transparent, self adhesive book covering material.

Apart from these furnishings there should be plenty of tables and chairs for the children who are working in the library. The chairs should be comfortable with padded seats but need not be selected from a specialist's catalogue as these tend to be expensive. Ordinary tables and chairs will suffice. A pair of steps for reaching high shelves will be useful. The librarian's table should be by the exit so that everyone taking out books must pass it and it should carry the book cards and tickets as well as the accessions register. If there is enough money available magazine holders for the various journals will help to preserve them and there should be files for pictures, press cuttings etc.

If prints or pictures are put up on the walls – some local libraries offer a lending service and there are a number of firms specializing in good cheap reproductions of famous prints and paintings – they should be changed at frequent intervals to make the room bright and interesting.

Some school libraries even include educational games and jigsaw puzzles among their accessories and these are greatly appreciated, especially by younger children and help to make the library both a focal point and a centre of activity.

Individual conditions will dictate the amount of space available but a library should have a ratio of about 3·7 square metres to each user, i.e. to each person studying in the library, and a minimum of 2·3 square metres per user has been laid down. Not every library will be able to allocate this space and common sense must see that senseless overcrowding is avoided. There should be adequate natural lighting and the artificial lighting should be sufficient to illuminate all the books in the library. The lighting should be strongest in the working section but individual table lamps are not recommended because of the danger of knocking them over or tripping over the flex.

Selection and purchase of books

The actual selection of suitable books will probably provide the teacher with one of the biggest headaches when it comes to organizing a school library. This depends so much upon individual factors, the amount of money available each year being of course one of the main limiting influences. A school which can afford £200 is obviously going to have a wider selection of books than one which has only £25 to spend.

Another point to be taken into account is the environment of the school. One with a predominantly middle class bias among its pupils will find a greater demand for rather more sophisticated books than a school in a working class area where books are not common at home.

In the same way local interests must be considered. When I taught at a Portsmouth school we found that the children would read almost anything about the navy and its history, while in a similar school in Westminster books about the Houses of Parliament were in great demand.

Keeping up to date with children's interests is another important factor. Any number of different spurs can stimulate children's curiosity – a television series, an important sporting event, news headlines and so on. Many if not most of these interests may well be fleeting, but a good teacher librarian will try to cater for them, if only by buying a few paperback books on the subject in question.

A great deal of research has been done into the subject of children's reading and it is generally agreed that in the pre-adolescent years there are a number of subjects which, if well enough treated, will usually appeal to boys and girls. This matter was summarized in *Surrounded by Books* by R. W. Purton (Ward Lock Educational 1962) when he published the results of a survey conducted among 1,250 London juniors as to the topics that interested them most. The first three places among fourth year children were as follows:

Boys		Girls	
1	sport	1	fairy tales
2	true adventure	2	true adventure
3	legends	3	legends

Other surveys, among them *What do Boys and Girls Read?* by A. J. Jenkinson (Methuen 1940), *About Books for Children* by D. N. White (OUP 1946) and the writings of Margery Fisher and others indicate that subjects favoured by children include suspense, adventure, stories of home life, history, crime, animals, travel, exploration, careers, do it yourself, biography and background.

There are many books on the market dealing with the subjects listed above and many others as well but not all of them are well written or well produced. It is the task of the teacher to separate the wheat from the chaff.

There are certain things to look for in the content of any book. In *Libraries for Children* Lionel McColvin has listed these as 'substance, sincerity, truth, right attitudes, good writing, accuracy and being up to date', and these are virtues to be sought in any book for children or adults. Physically a book ought to look bright and pleasant, it should be written on good quality paper with clear well set type and good, relevant illustrations and the book should not be overpriced.

There is little doubt, however, that too many books for children are mediocre. Eleanor Graham makes this point in *Junior Bookshelf* when she writes:

> We need far more truth in children's books; far greater truth in characterization and about human relationships between adult and adult, and adult and child, as well as between children. We need to tell more of the truth about the world and the way men live in it, the work they do and what it feels like to be doing it; about the everyday occupations as well as those which promise adventure, and particularly about those first jobs to which many readers will be looking forward. . . .[2]

In order to find the truth advocated by Miss Graham some teachers will turn to the classics of children's literature but whether these classics should be kept in a school library is another vexed point. Many teachers feel that no infant school library would be complete without a set of books by Beatrix Potter, just as the junior section should contain *Treasure Island* and *The Black Arrow* and the senior shelves must house the works of Charles Dickens. Others may agree with Ernest Roe when he writes in *Teachers, Librarians and Children*:

> Again, considerable damage is done with the best of intentions. Teachers who, whether in frank ignorance of any other children's books or disguising that ignorance as a virtue, recommend the classics to children may be given credit for their desire to hold high the banner of quality; they may genuinely believe that there are no better or more suitable books, that children should love in the 1960s what they themselves loved in the 1950s, 1940s or 1930s, that by reading such books and only such books may they be saved from the seductions of television; and sometimes, perhaps, with a child here and a child there, this blind optimism or desperate hope – it may be either – is justified. But what is the effect on the other 90 or 95 or 99 per cent of children?[3]

It is undeniably true that no matter how smart or comfortable the library room is it will make no difference to the children if they feel that the books it contains are uninteresting or irrelevant. Ruth Viguers makes this point in *Margin for Surprise*:

If we persist in giving children vocabularized books, patterned writing, informational books that answer all their questions before they are asked; if we pay too much attention to the tricks used to make books sell rather than to the contents of books; if we do not make easily available the stories and books that give children the adventures and exciting experiences they want, they will reject books.[4]

From what has been written so far the teacher librarian might well suppose that there are more negative than positive aspects about selecting books for the library in a school. The real answer of course is that the library should contain a wide selection of all types of books. Children who prefer the classics may then read them, while those who prefer less elevating material may read that and perhaps progress later to better books.

Much depends upon the teacher's power of selection. It should be remembered that he is selecting books, not collecting them, and so he is constantly faced with a number of choices. In the final analysis, if money is in short supply, priority must be given to books that the teacher librarian knows the children will turn to first.

It may be argued that the children will turn first to the gaudy and trivial and up to a point this is correct, but many librarians feel that after a time children will grow tired of third rate reading matter and look for something better. In *About Books for Children* Dorothy Neal White writes:

In my experience as a children's librarian I have found that good books drive out bad.[5]

This is not to say that children will inevitably turn to what we regard as good books straight away, but even so inferior popular books have their place in a school library as Eric Leyland points out in *Libraries in Schools* when he says:

. . . one must consider the possibility that even the most trivial piece of fiction may become valuable not intrinsically but because of the result it achieves. It frequently happens that a boy or girl who has hitherto shown no interest in reading, or perhaps evinced a definite dislike for books, may by reason of fortuitously alighting on the trivial story acquire a taste for reading and be persuaded to indulge further and to better effect.[6]

The teacher's own knowledge of the children in the school, their interests and abilities, will be called upon when it comes to selecting books for their library. It will help if the teacher notices the sort of books the children are bringing to school and reading. A chat with the local librarian may also be of assistance in determining just what most children in the area seem to enjoy in the way of books.

Another method of keeping in touch is to read the various magazines specializing in reviews of children's books – a list is given later in the chapter – and making notes of the recommended ones.

Catalogues issued by the publishers will supply details of the books they issue, but the descriptions are hardly likely to be unbiased and the teacher is advised to send for specimen copies before ordering. All the same the teacher librarian should try to get on the mailing list of the various publishers and to file their catalogues in the library, replacing them when they get out of date.

A good way of viewing a wide selection of books for children is to visit the exhibitions sponsored by such organizations as the NUT and the NAS. Most publishers take stands at such exhibitions and their representatives are pleased to display a selection of their books and to answer questions about them

Full use must also be made of other members of the staff, especially subject specialists, who should be asked to supply lists of recommended reading in their own particular field.

It should be mentioned in passing that it is not always a good idea to select books for the school library based on a list of what the local bookshop is selling. In many cases only the more sophisticated parents seem to give books as presents and the children who receive them are hardly representative. Another drawback is that parents do not always buy their children the sort of books that the children want.

Each age range presents its own individual problems to the teacher librarian. At the infant stage there is the problem of the initial teaching alphabet. If the children in the school are learning to read through i ta then books written in i ta must be included in the school library. Among the better series using this method are *Many Cargoes* (Evans), *McKee Reading Scheme* (Nelson), *Père Castor Books* (Initial Teaching Publishing) and the *Yellow Door Stories* (Methuen).

At the junior school level the teacher will soon learn to recognize the names of those authors whose books always seem to hold children and I have tried to make a list of them at the end of this chapter. It should be remembered, as Mary Atkinson writes in *Junior School Community*:

. . . the junior school is not a place for the study of literature. It is enjoyment of a story for the sake of the story, not for interest in the development of character and ideals, that these children desire.[7]

The Reading
Corner

It is nice to be quiet here.

Buy
more
fruit.

We went out
in our boat.
The sea was
so rough we
had to turn
back.   Peter

funnel

anchor

A spare corner in the classroom can easily be adapted to form a library
area where children can read quietly

A project displayed in the classroom is a useful way of introducing children to the reference books to be found in the school library

They also desire information about the world in which they live and they should be able to turn to the school library for this information suitably housed in the shelves under the relevant headings of natural history, geography, travel and exploration etc. At the senior level the selection of books becomes even more difficult. In *The Disappearing Dais* Frank Whitehead writes:

> Some teachers try to influence their pupils' choice of books by issuing lists of recommended library reading for each form or year, but it is not uncommon to find that they are largely ignored by the children for whom they are intended. We have to reckon with the fact that children at this stage want to be independent in their choice of reading material and like to feel that in this area of their lives at least they can keep control in their own hands.[8]

To provide lists of books for senior children (as opposed to lists for teachers seeking guidance in stocking a library) is of little use anyway because as W. D. Wall points out in *The Adolescent Child*:

> All the researches which have been made into adolescent reading tastes tend to the conclusion that by the age of fifteen or sixteen generalizations such as could have been made in the years of childhood are no longer possible, and much the same range and variety of interests is apparent in an adolescent group as among adults.[9]

In short, when it comes to providing books for a school library the teacher should provide as wide a selection as possible. There should be emphasis on the sort of book the teacher knows will appeal to the children in his school, but he should not rule out books which at first glance might seem of no interest. As a general rule if a book is well enough written it should be included, finance permitting, because one day a child might turn to it and be persuaded to start reading.

The tricky question of censorship must also be considered. Today with sex and violence freely discussed and illustrated in films, on television and in paperback books and magazines there might seem to be a case for relaxing standards in the school library and including books that some might consider permissive. The teacher librarian must remember that he stands in *loco parentis* to the children using the library and must consider whether he would allow his own children access to some of the books available in the publishers' catalogues. The matter of deciding which books are good and bad is far from easy and one can only echo the words of Eric Leyland in *Libraries in Schools* when he says:

There is little to assist the teacher librarian, except an awareness of his inescapable responsibility and a realization that this must be practised within the framework of the world today rather than of yesterday.[10]

A good school library will be run by a committee which can discuss any books whose suitability has been queried. The composition of such a committee varies from school to school but should include the teacher librarian, the headmaster or deputy headmaster, other interested members of the staff and, certainly in senior schools, one or two prefects. This committee should also be responsible for staffing the library. This will include drawing up a list of monitors, arranging for them to be instructed in their duties and giving them stated times at which to perform them. Under the supervision of the librarian the monitors should be responsible for maintaining order in the library, seeing that it is kept clean, issuing and accepting books and stocktaking once a year. When it is time for stocktaking all books should be called in and checked against the lists. Whenever a book is ordered it should be written down in an accessions register or on an accessions card, given a number which is written down in the book when it arrives, the dust jacket displayed on the 'New Books' notice board and the book put on the appropriate shelf.

If there is enough money available a supply of bookplates bearing the name of the school should be ordered and one bookplate gummed into each book. Periodically all books should be checked for damage and torn pages gummed together. When the condition of a book is such that it is beyond repair it should be withdrawn from the shelves.

Budget permitting, a certain sum should be earmarked for magazines as well as books. The best book cannot remain up to date indefinitely and a constant supply of magazines will do a great deal towards satisfying the search for knowledge and information.

When it comes to ordering the books needed for the school library the teacher librarian will need to use the catalogues issued by the different publishing firms supplying books for children. In the lists of recommended books at the end of this chapter the names of the relevant publishers are given but these are by no means the only ones supplying books for children and teachers are advised to send for the catalogues of all the main firms before ordering books. When it comes to books that are out of copyright – *Treasure Island* etc – more than one publisher might issue it and teachers will want to compare prices and standards.

Books may be ordered direct from the publisher but it should be remembered that library books are usually ordered singly, not in sets of thirty or forty as is the case with textbooks. Thus if twenty different library books are ordered ten or more different publishers may be involved and in a case of this sort it will be better to make the order through a local bookseller. The Net Book Agreement now in force forbids booksellers to reduce the selling price of net books but teachers should keep themselves informed of the situation in case discounts may be obtained on large orders from booksellers or from wholesalers.

Cataloguing and classifying books

Unless the school library is quickly to degenerate into a shambles an efficient method of cataloguing and classifying the books must be found. There are a number of accepted methods but the one most generally used in all kinds of libraries is that known as the Dewey Decimal Classification. Full details of this system may be found in the *Dewey Decimal Classification and Relative Index* published by the Forest Press of New York who hold the copyright on the system and the method is also described in some detail in *Using Your Library* by E. Grimshaw (E. J. Arnold 1963), *Introduction to Dewey Decimal Classification for British Schools* compiled by Marjorie Chambers (Gresswell 1961) and in *Teach Yourself Librarianship* Barbara Kyle (EUP 1964).

The Dewey system was first published in 1876 and is still one of the best and simplest of classification methods, although some teachers may prefer to adapt it slightly according to the prevailing conditions. Briefly, the Dewey system divides books into ten main headings according to subject matter and then into subheadings under each main heading. Each main group has ten subgroups.

The various divisions are as follows:

900 History, geography and travel (subdivided into regions – European history etc)
800 Literature (subdivided into various regions – American literature etc)
700 The arts (subdivided into painting, sculpture etc)
600 Technology (subdivided into engineering, agriculture etc)
500 Science (subdivided into pure science, mathematics etc)
400 Language (subdivided into English language, Germanic languages etc)
300 Social sciences (subdivided into statistics, economics etc)
200 Religion (subdivided into Bible, Devotional theology etc)
100 Philosophy (subdivided into metaphysics, logic etc)
000 General works (subdivided into encyclopedias etc)

In an article in *Teachers World* R. W. Purton explains how he has adapted this system to suit a junior school library:

Instead of having a set of shelves headed nature and nothing else, one now has a set of shelves still headed nature but with a valuable subclassification in that all books on nature study will be numbered 574, flowers 582, insects 595, birds 598 and animals 599, to mention only a few.[11]

If all non fiction books in the library are catalogued in this fashion and allocated space among the shelves then returning the books to the correct places will present no problems and finding a book will be made much easier. Mr Purton suggests that for younger readers the system be further simplified by the use of a different colour for each section of shelving – red for scripture, blue for science, and so on and I have used this method with considerable success in primary schools.

Once the books have been classified and allocated their positions on the shelves it is essential to catalogue them so that they may be found with a minimum of fuss and trouble. The best way to do this is to have a catalogue cabinet in the library. Every time a new book is added its particulars are written on small card and the card put in the cabinet.

If possible it is better to have two catalogues rather than one. One cabinet contains cards with the names of the authors of books in the library and is known as the author catalogue. The other cabinet contains the titles of the books and is known as the title catalogue. If the librarian has time to make out a third subject catalogue then a really effective cross reference system will result.

In the author catalogue the cards are filed under the names of the authors in alphabetical order. Each card contains the name of the author, the title of the book and the classification number. For example *Animals of Canada* by Peter Allen would be filed in the author catalogue as:

Allen, Peter   Animals of Canada   Cat no 599

In the title catalogue this book would be filed as

Animals of Canada   by Peter Allen   Cat no 599

In the subject catalogue it would be filed as

Animals   Animals of Canada   by Peter Allen   Cat no 599

Some librarians prefer to use a combined author and title catalogue. This entails making out two cards for each book, one under the author's name and one under the title of the book, and putting them alphabetically in the same file as a double check.

In all files it will be a great help to insert tabs marked A, B, C etc among the cards and so divide them up in alphabetical order and make it easier to find the individual cards. Some catalogue cabinets contain subdivisions; one will hold cards A – D, the next E – H etc while others merely hold all the cards in one large cabinet.

In all school libraries it will be a great help to the children if signs and diagrams on the walls explain how to find various books, the use of the classification system and so on. A chart showing the actual location of books by subject will be of great help.

Issuing books

It is important to introduce an efficient and secure system of issuing library books from the beginning. There are a number of ways of doing this but most methods are variations of one generally accepted system. This involves giving each child a personal library card or ticket (bearing his name, class and sometimes a reference number) which will be given up each time the child withdraws a book from the library. The ticket should be of the pocket or wallet type because a card from the borrowed book will be inserted into it. Similarly, each book should have a pocket glued inside the front or back cover in which a single card bearing the name of the book and the author, together with a reference number, should be kept. The reference number will also be permanently marked in the book, usually on a page stuck in to receive the date stamp.

When a child has selected a book he takes it to the librarian together with his personal library ticket. The librarian takes out the card from the book and stamps the appropriate page with the date by which the book has to be returned–usually a fortnight later. The librarian must remember to put the date stamp forward one day first thing each morning. The librarian then takes the personal library ticket from the child and inserts the book ticket into the wallet and files it in a cabinet under the day on which the book was borrowed. When the child returns the book the librarian sees from the date stamp the day on which the book was withdrawn, checks the reference number on the book with the reference number inserted in the personal ticket filed in the cabinet, returns the book card to the book, gives the child his personal ticket and allows him to select another book.

A system of fines should be drawn up to dissuade children from keeping books too long and if time allows the books should be examined quickly when they are returned to ensure that they are in good condition. When enough books have been returned they can be sorted out into rough order, placed on the book trolley and returned to their correct places on the shelves.

Some books should not be allowed out of the library i.e. expensive reference books – encyclopedias and the like – which should always be available on the shelves.

Teaching children to use the library

Once the books have been selected, the equipment installed and a simple classification and cataloguing system adopted, the children should be encouraged to use the library and to make themselves familiar with it. They should be made to feel from the start that they are welcome to use its facilities but they must always be taught that both the books and the room must be treated with respect. Any rules that have been drawn up must be obeyed, times of opening and closing observed and so on.

This means that the teacher librarian must see to it that the children are taught how to use the library. A certain amount can be done in the library itself as has already been suggested e.g. the classification and cataloguing system explained, diagrams of the shelving arrangements displayed etc. In the library however both teacher and children will be too busy actually using the books to have much time for explanations and discussions, and a great deal more can be done in the classroom.

If the teacher who is acting as the librarian takes a number of different classes in the school then the problem is solved because he or she can use some of these periods to teach the children about the library and how to use it properly. If this is not practicable then other teachers on the staff must play their part in indoctrinating the students. N. M. Butterworth makes this point in an article when he writes:

> Ideally the basic introduction to the library ought to be given during the first two or three weeks that a pupil is in school. One should devote not one but several periods a week to library instruction. Since it is most unlikely that the teacher librarian will be able to conduct introductory work for several classes simultaneously even if such an arrangement were desirable, the task must be left with the teachers of English. A course of library skills can form the major portion of work in English during the first week or two of term. In this way the library is soon available as a resource for all teachers at a time when enthusiasm is still high.[12]

The contents of these library periods will vary from class to class but they should contain instruction on how to handle books properly, how to return them to the correct places on the shelves, how to use the catalogues, how to use the various reference books and how to take a book out of the library. If any new books are added to the library the fact should be made known to the children and, if possible, a description of the book given, perhaps in a duplicated sheet handed round or pinned up on classroom walls.

The children should also be made aware of the alternative roles of the library – as a centre for project and topic activities, as a display centre for wall newspapers and art and craft work etc. Older children should be allowed to volunteer for duty as assistant librarians and initiated further into the intricacies of cataloguing and classification. All children should know the opening and closing times of the library in the lunch hour and after school. Needless to say the library will grow in prestige and attract more visitors if it can be used as a centre for displays and exhibitions of various sorts.

Coordination with other libraries

Even when there is an efficient school library it is still a good idea to maintain class libraries, especially in infant and junior schools. This will encourage children to read and accustom them to borrowing and looking after books. No elaborate system of booking out need be introduced; the names of books and borrowers may be entered in an exercise book and a monitor put in charge of loans. At this stage teachers can introduce instruction in the make up of a book, explaining to the children the function of such things as the title page, name of the publisher, use of the index etc.

It is hoped that the teacher librarian will coordinate as far as possible with the local public library, especially with the junior section. Services available vary from area to area. In one area in which I taught the local library even lent prints and paintings to primary and secondary schools in addition to sending round a mobile library two or three times a year to the schools. Often librarians are prepared to come and talk to the children about books and libraries and the facilities available locally.

An excellent pamphlet giving details of the range of facilities provided by the public library service has been issued by the Department of Education and Science under the heading Report on Education No 54: of *The Public Library Service and You* (1969) and teachers are recommended to try and obtain a copy.

At the moment there are 385 library authorities in England and 40 in Wales, who between them issue about 500 million books per year. Such libraries perform many helpful duties in the field of education as *Public Libraries and Education* points out:

Students in schools, colleges and universities usually have access to their own libraries, but these and public libraries are becoming complementary to each other as fruitful links are established between them. The professional librarian is usually both able and willing to give practical help and technical advice to teachers on running school libraries. Librarians also help teachers in the exacting task of selecting books from the 3,000 or so children's books published annually. This is particularly the case where the public library provides, on behalf of the local education authority, a proportion of the school library books. Guidance may be offered to teachers in the form of annotated book lists or by maintaining standing exhibitions of suitable books in print. This guidance together with occasional discussions between teachers and librarians helps to ensure that school library funds are spent to the best advantage.[13]

Other ways in which the public library service may assist students is by providing reference services in local public libraries, museums and art galleries. When the local library finds itself unable to provide the books required it will know where to obtain the book from the vast network of local, national and specialist libraries in Great Britain.

Summary
Starting and running a school library is not a difficult task once the basic knowledge has been acquired and the results of maintaining such a service will certainly make up for the amount of time and trouble spent in the process.

The most important point as far as the children are concerned is to ensure that they know how to use the library to its best advantage. Those teachers who want to give their children plenty of practice in looking things up and making themselves familiar with books and libraries are recommended to read *Library Assignments* by M. Howard (Edward Arnold 1968 – Teachers' Book supplied). The pupils work through the book assignment by assignment and it is suitable for top juniors and most secondary school students.

Book lists
To help the beginner librarian select books for the school library the following book lists are included. They do not pretend to be comprehensive but I have found myself that they have been popular with the respective age ranges for which they are intended. The series mentioned are well produced and sturdy and should stand up to a great deal of wear and tear.

The infant school library (5–7 years)
Teachers wishing to select books for children in the 5–7 age range are recommended to read *The Way of the Storyteller* by Ruth Sawyer (Bodley Head 1966) and *A Storyteller's Choice* by Eileen Colwell (Bodley Head 1963). Books which I have always found to be well produced and suitable in every way for infants are listed below.

Series
Beginner Books Collins; *Beginning to Read Books* Benn; *Candy Books* Nelson; *Children's Bible Stories* Nelson; *Cock Robin Classics* Blackie; *The Children's Bookshelf* Harrap; *The Dragonfly Story Books* Wheaton; *Favourite Books* Nelson; *Favourite Fairy Tales* Bodley Head; Andrew Lang *Fifty Favourite Fairy Tales* Bodley Head; *First Bible Stories* Blackie; *First of All* Nelson; *Minibooks* Collins; *Mouse Books* Methuen; *Muller Easy Readers* Muller; *New Easy to Read* Blackie; *Our Animal Story Books* Harrap; *The Pleasure Books* Wheaton; *The Red Bus* Nelson; *Robin Bible Story Books* Longacre Press; *Springboard Readers* Warne; *Topsy and Tim* Blackie.

Fiction
Writing for children in the infant school range is a difficult business and few authors manage to rise above the merely competent in this field. Among those I have always found popular with younger children are:

Edward Ardizzone *Little Tim and the Brave Sea Captain* etc OUP

Helen Bannerman *The Story of Little Black Sambo* etc Chatto and Windus

Roger Duvoisin *Petunia* etc Bodley Head

Rumer Godden *The Mousewife* etc Macmillan

Anita Hewett *The Little White Hen* etc Bodley Head

Andrew Lang *Fifty Favourite Fairy Tales* etc Bodley Head

A. A. Milne *When We Were Young* etc Methuen

Beatrix Potter *The Tale of Peter Rabbit* etc Warne

Diana Ross *The Little Red Engine* etc Faber

Dr Seuss *And To Think That I Saw It On Mulberry Street* etc Vanguard Press

Margery Sharp *The Rescuers* etc Collins

William Stobbs *The Golden Goose* etc Bodley Head

Eve Titus *Anatole* etc Bodley Head

Alison Uttley *Little Grey Rabbit* etc Collins

Brian Wildsmith *The Lion and the Rat* etc OUP

Verse
Percy Buck *The Oxford Nursery Song Book* OUP

Barbara Ireson *The Faber Book of Nursery Verse* Faber

The junior school library (7–11 years)
The following books are recommended for consideration by any teacher wishing to start collecting books for a junior school library. As there would not be enough space to mention all the individual books

worthy of choice, I have in many cases indicated specific *series* of books which I have always found to have a high content and production standard.

Encyclopedias and works of reference
Gerald E. Speck and John Hetherington *Animal Wonderland* Ward Lock; J. L. Klink *The Bible for Children* Burke; *Bible Readings for Boys and Girls* Nelson; *Black's Children's Encyclopedia* (2 volumes) A. and C. Black; S. Johnson *The Children's Dictionary* Wheaton; Luana M. Wells *The Children's Garden* Nelson; *Eagle Book of Hobbies* Longacre Press; W. D. Wright *First Encyclopedia* Nisbet; *Girl Book of Hobbies* Longacre Press; *The Holy Bible* (authorized version or revised standard version) Collins; G. Palmer *The Junior Bible Encyclopedia* Burke; Gerald E. Speck *Junior Pictorial Encyclopedia* Ward Lock; Gerald E. Speck *Junior Pictorial Encyclopedia of Science* Ward Lock; *The Oxford Atlas* OUP; *The Oxford Junior Encyclopedia* (13 volumes) OUP; *Reader's Digest Complete Atlas of the British Isles* Collins Longmans; *World Book Encyclopedia* Field Enterprises.

The world around us
The Burke Book Of series (*Astronomy, Buses of the World* etc) Burke; *Do You Know?* series (*Reptiles, The Solar System* etc) Collins; *Lively Youngsters* series (*Everyday Things for Lively Youngsters* etc) Cassell; *Looking and Finding* series (*On A Railway Journey, On The Farm* etc) Ward Lock Educational; *Our World* series (*What Happens Underground, What Happens in the Sea* etc) Macmillan; *The Study Books* series (*The Land, Maps* etc) Collins; *Topic Books* series (*Birds, Motor Cars* etc) Ward Lock Educational.

Myths, legends and traditional tales
James Reeves *Aesop's Fables* Blackie
Rosemary Sutcliff *Beowulf* Bodley Head
Joseph Jacobs *English Fairy Tales* Muller
Hans Andersen *Fairy Tales and Legends* Bodley Head
Wilhelm Matthiessen *Folk Tales* Burke
Anne Terry White *Golden Treasury of Myths and Legends* Paul Hamlyn
Roger Lancelyn Green *Heroes of Greece and Troy* Bodley Head
E. M. Almedingen *The Knights of the Round Table* Bodley Head
Robert Graves *Myths of Ancient Greece* Cassell
Roger Lancelyn Green *Myths of the Norsemen* Bodley Head
Myths and Legends series (*Ancient Greece and Rome, Babylon and Persia*) Burke

Andrew Lang *Tales from the Arabian Nights* Longmans Green
Sorche Nic Leodhas *Thistle and Thyme* Bodley Head
F. M. Pilkington *Shamrock and Spear* Bodley Head
Joel Chandler Harris *Uncle Remus* Routledge

Biographies
Blackie Biographies series (*Abraham Lincoln, Magellan* etc) Blackie;
Living Names series (*Seven Inventors, Six Good Samaritans* etc) OUP; *Lives
of Great Men and Women* series (*Social Reformers, Great Explorers* etc)
OUP; Macdonald Hastings *More Men of Glory* Longacre Press; *Nelson's
Picture Biographies* (*William Shakespeare, Buffalo Bill* etc) Nelson; *Path-
finder Biographies* (*Aristotle, Marconi* etc) Weidenfeld and Nicolson.

History
Caravel series (*Captain Cook and the South Pacific, Alexander the Great*)
Cassell; Molly Harrison *Children in History* Hulton; M. and C. H. B.
Quennell *Everyday Life* series Batsford; *Finding Out* series (*The Romans,
The Trojans*) Muller; *Junior Reference* series (*A History of Houses, Travel
by Road* etc) Black; *Past into Present* series (*Home, Life, Poverty* etc)
Batsford; *People of the Past* series (*A Soldier on Hadrian's Wall, A Saxon
Settler* etc) OUP; *The St George's Library* series (*Vikings at Home and
Abroad, The Story of Rome* etc) Arnold; *Topics Through Time* series (*The
Housewife, The Inventor* etc) ULP.

Geography and travel
Animals of the World OUP; *Children Near and Far* series (*Toto Joins the
Fishermen* etc) Hulton; *Family* series (*A Family in Greece, A Family in
Samoa* etc) Hulton; *How People Live* series (*How People Live in Norway*
etc) Ward Lock Educational; *Let's Visit Series* (*Let's Visit Australia, Let's
Visit India* etc) Burke; *Many Cargoes* series (*Grain, Sugar* etc) Evans;
My Home series (*My Home in India* etc) Longmans Green; *Panorama*
series Collins; *Young* series (*Young Japan, Young India* etc) Wheaton.

Natural history
George C. Goodwin *Small Mammals* Ward Lock; *Birds* series (*The
Robin, The Swallow* etc) Longmans; *Making and Keeping* series (*A Box
Garden, An Aquarium* etc) Ward Lock Educational; *Natural Science
Picture Books* Bodley Head; *Nature's Ways* series Hulton; *Pet and Live-
stock* series (*Ducks and Geese, Your Dog* etc) Cassell; *Read about Nature*
series (*Bats, Owls and Badgers* etc) Wheaton; *Studying Nature* series
Evans; *We Animals* series (*Animals in Their Homes* etc) Nelson.

Careers

People at Work series (*Building, Car Making* etc) Blackie; *People's Jobs* series (*The Coal Miner, The Fireman* etc) Ward Lock Educational.

Poetry

R. L. Stevenson *A Child's Garden of Verses* Collins
Eleanor Farjeon *A Thread of Gold* Bodley Head
Leonard Clark *Drums and Trumpets* Bodley Head
John Smith *My Kind of Verse* Burke
J. Murray Macbain *The Book of a Thousand Poems* Evans

Science

Do You Know About series (*The Earth, The Stars*) Collins; *Finding Out About Science* series (*The Telephone, Engines* etc) Weidenfeld and Nicolson; *Junior Science* series (*Volcanoes, Weather Experiments* etc) Muller; *Simple Science* series (*Sleep* etc) World's Work.

Religion

Mary Devitt *Bible Stories* Macmillan
N. J. Bull *Children of the Bible* Evans
Collins' Scripture Colour Books Macmillan
B. C. Krall *Stories of Favourite Saints* REP

Fiction

There are many thousands of books for primary school children which could be listed under this title. Space will not allow a detailed list so a number of recommended series have been given.

Acorn Library Collins; *Antelope Books* Hamish Hamilton; *Brock Books* Brockhampton Press; Frank Richards *Billy Bunter* series Cassell; *Enid Blyton's Junior Story Books* Collins; *Gazelle Books* Hamish Hamilton; *The Haldon Children's Fiction Library* Wheaton; Anthony Buckeridge *Jennings* series Collins; Michael Bond *Paddington* series Collins; *Puffin Books* Penguin; *Rainbow Books* Ward Lock; *Seven to Ten Stories* Blackie; *Seagull Library* Collins; *Wren Books* Burke.

Most teachers will have their own list of authors who usually appeal to children. Here are some of the writers whose books have almost always appealed to the primary school children I have taught.

Eric Allen *Pepe Moreno* etc Faber
Enid Blyton *The Boy Next Door* etc Angus and Robertson
Hilda Boden *Peter and Pippin* etc Wheaton
Alan Boucher *The Hornstranders* etc Constable
Lewis Carroll *Alice's Adventures in Wonderland* etc Macmillan

Carlo Collodi *Pinocchio* etc Dent
Mary Cockett *Acrobat Hamster* Hamish Hamilton
Eleanor Farjeon *Jim at the Corner* etc OUP
Alan Garner *The Owl Service* etc Collins
Kenneth Grahame *The Reluctant Dragon* etc Collins
Kathleen Hale *Orlando's Magic Carpet* etc Murray
Molly Hunter *Thomas and the Warlock* etc Blackie
Alan Jenkins *White Horses and Black Bulls* etc Blackie
Rudyard Kipling *Just So Stories* etc Macmillan
Hugh Lofting *Dr Doolittle* etc Cape
William Mayne *A Grass Rope* etc OUP
A. A. Milne *Winnie the Pooh* etc Methuen
Mary Norton *The Borrowers* etc Dent
Philippa Pearce *Mrs Cockle's Cat* etc Constable
Sheena Porter *Nordy Bank* etc OUP
Gerald Raferty *Snow Cloud, Stallion* Penguin
Jack Schaefer *Old Ramon* etc Deutsch
Noel Streatfeild *The Circus is Coming* etc Dent
Grace Skaar *A Boy and His Horse* etc Hamish Hamilton
Rosemary Sutcliff *The Queen Elizabeth Story* etc OUP
P. L. Travers *Mary Poppins* etc Collins
Joyce Towers *The Seaside Donkey* etc Brockhampton Press

The secondary school (comprehensive and grammar) library (12–16 years)

Again reliable series of books are given rather than individual titles in most cases, as well as a number of authors popular with boys and girls in this age range.

Reference and background books

L. H. Grollenberg *Atlas of the Bible* Nelson; A. A. M. van der Heyden and H. H. Scullard *Atlas of the Classical World* Nelson; B. Ernst and Tj de Vries *Atlas of the Universe* Nelson; *Bible Anthology* Dent; E. C. Brewer *Brewer's Dictionary of Phrase and Fable* Cassell; *Chambers's Twentieth Century Dictionary* Chambers; *Chambers's World Gazetteer and Geographical Dictionary* Chambers; *Concise Oxford Dictionary* Oxford; *Dictionary of Quotations* Nelson; *Encyclopedia Britannica*; *The Holy Bible* (authorized version or standard revised version) Collins; H. L. Gee *Nelson's Encyclopedia* Nelson; *Oxford Junior Encyclopedia* OUP; William Shakespeare *Plays* Dent; *Standard Encyclopedia* series Weidenfeld and Nicolson.

Geography

Challenge Books series Chatto and Windus; *Essential Geography* (*Clothing, Food* etc) Hulton; *The Faber Atlas* Faber; *How People Live* series (*The Sudan* etc) Ward Lock Educational; *Let's Visit* series (*Let's Visit Italy, Let's Visit Germany* etc) Burke; *Let's Travel* series (*Let's Travel in France* etc) Odhams; *Men at Work* series (*Textiles. Coal* etc) Longmans; *New Visual Geography* series (*Ice Cap and Tundra* etc) Hutchinson; *Physical Geography* series (*Beaches and Coastlines* etc) Hulton; *Portraits of Cities* series (*Athens, London*) Lutterworth; *Reference Geographies* series (*Water and Man* etc) Chatto and Windus; *Rivers of the World* series (*The Seine* etc) Muller; *Stories of Industry* series (*Glass, Iron and Steel* etc) Warne.

History

English Life series (*Life in Roman Britain* etc) Batsford; G. M. Trevelyan *Illustrated English Social History* Penguin; *Know About* series (*Know About the Crusades* etc) Blackie; *Picture History* series (*The Cinema, Flight* etc) Longacre Press; *Then and There* series (*Ancient Egypt, The Vikings* etc) Longmans; *Twentieth Century History Topics* (*Adolf Hitler and Modern Germany* etc) Cassell; *Sources of History* series (*The English Poor Law* etc) Macmillan; *The Story Of* series (*The Story of Greece* etc) Nelson; *What Became of ?* series (*What Became of the Maya* etc) Wheaton; *The Young Historian* series (*Ancient Persia* etc) Weidenfeld and Nicolson.

Natural history

George C. Goodwin *Small Mammals* Ward Lock; *Children's Book Of* series (*Children's Book of British Birds* etc) Chambers; *Field Guides* (*Nest Boxes* etc) British Trust for Ornithology; *Life Nature Library* series (*The Reptiles* etc) Time-Life International; *Living Universe* series (*The Animal World* etc) Nelson; *Natural History* series (*The Life of Plants*) Weidenfeld and Nicolson; *Nature Rambles* series (*Winter to Spring* etc) Warne; *New Naturalist* series (*Folklore of Birds* etc) Collins; *Visual* series (*Life in Freshwater* etc) OUP; *Wildlife* series (*Wildlife in Canada* etc) Macmillan; *World of Nature* series (*A Bird is Born* etc) Oliver and Boyd; *Young Specialist* series (*Trees, Weather* etc) Burke.

Biography

Constable Young Books series (*Von Humboldt, Scientist, Explorer, Adventurer* etc) Constable; *History Through Great Lives* series (*William Caxton to Captain Cook* etc) Cassell; *Leaders of Religion* series (*John Wesley* etc) Nelson; *Pathfinder Biographies* (*James Watt* etc) Weidenfeld and Nicolson; *Red Lion Lives* (*Sir Alexander Fleming* etc) Cassell; *World* series (*Shakespeare and His World* etc) Lutterworth.

Science

Finding Out About Science series (*Light and Colour, Germs* etc) Weidenfeld and Nicolson; *Science in Industry* series (*Oil, Electricity* etc) Burke; *Science on the March* series (*The Air and You* etc) Longmans; *Science Study* series (*The Neutron Story* etc) Heinemann: *Story of Electricity* series (*The Atom* etc) Blackwell; *Story of Life* series (*Growing and Moving* etc) Blackwell.

Religion and morals

Everyday Life series (*Everyday Life in Old Testament Times* etc) Batsford; *Landmarks in the Story of Christianity* series (*The Plans of Jesus* etc) Macmillan; *Discussion* series Ward Lock Educational; John Elliott *Me, Other People and God* Mowbray; James Cartman *Men and Their Religions* Harrap; N. J. Bull *The Rise of the Church* Heinemann.

Hobbies, sports and pastimes

The Beeton Homebooks series (*Cakes and Pastries* etc) Ward Lock; *Canoeing* series (*Choosing a Canoe and its Equipment* etc) British Canoe Union; J. T. Hankinson *Cricket for Schools* Allen and Unwin; J. G. Cone *Book of Handicrafts* Warne; L. Scrivener *The Complete Ballroom Dancer* Evans; *Farming and Gardening* series (*The Cassell Book of Farm Study* etc) Cassell; *Make your Own* series (*Make Your Own Model Village* etc) Nelson; *Model Maker* series (*Model Aeroplanes* etc) Cassell; A. L. Colbeck *Modern Basketball* Kaye and Ward; G. Rébuffat *On Snow and Rock* Kaye and Ward; *Step by Step* series (*Making Furniture* etc) Warne; Dennis Law *Tackle Soccer this Way* Stanley Paul; *Teach Yourself* series (*Hockey* etc) EUP; *Young Sportsman's Library* (*Bowling, Golf* etc) Nelson; *Young Sportsman* series (*Batting, Spin Bowling* etc) Phoenix House.

Fiction

Choosing suitable books of fiction for the secondary age range is not an easy task. Teachers are recommended to study the lists of novels recommended on pp 65–68 and 83–84 of *The Disappearing Dais* by Frank Whitehead (Chatto and Windus 1966) for a comprehensive and extremely well selected list of books. Another book that the teacher should read is *Written for Children* by John Rowe Townsend (Miller 1965). Two books which are a little dated now but still worth reading are *What Do Boys and Girls Read?* by A. J. Jenkinson (Methuen 1940) and *About Books for Children* by D. N. White (OUP 1946).

For practical help in selecting suitable works of fiction teachers are urged to make themselves familiar with the publications of the National Book League. The National Book League has issued a number of descriptive pamphlets under the general heading of the *School Library*

Fiction series. Some individual titles in this very useful series are *Historical Fiction, Children and Adults, Mystery and Adventure, Children of Other Lands, Animal Stories, Fantasy, After Thirteen – Books for Teenagers.* In each pamphlet over 150 books are recommended, plots are given and the names of publishers, dates of publication, prices, etc are supplied. The pamphlets may be purchased from the National Book League, 7 Albemarle Street, Piccadilly, London WIX 4BB.

Keeping up to date with children's fiction is another problem to be faced. The teacher may overcome this to a certain extent by reading the various journals and magazines which give a reliable and unbiased review of children's fiction. These include *Growing Point* (edited by Margery Fisher), *Books for Your Children* (edited by Anne Wood), *Junior Bookshelf, School Librarian, Times Educational Supplement, Times Literary Supplement, Books and Bookmen, Teachers World* etc. For children's books from the USA the following journals publish frequent reviews: *Horn Book Magazine, Books for the Teenage, Standard Catalogue for High School Libraries* and the Bulletin of the Centre for Children's Books from the USA. In Australia the *Australian Book Review* publishes an annual children's supplement and *Books for Children* issued by the Children's Book Council of Victoria is strongly recommended.

Some of the problems of selecting works of fiction for the secondary school library have been touched upon earlier, in particular the problem of classics and of changing taste among children in the 12 – 16 + age range and I shall not go into them again here. Most of the classics may be found in two series – *Literature of Today and Yesterday* and *Kings Treasuries of Literature* – both published by Dent. Many other publishers also put out editions of famous books, among the better produced are those issued by Macdonald, Collins and Methuen.

Moving on to more modern authors, I have found the following writers to be popular with comprehensive and secondary modern children I have taught in various areas:

Richard Armstrong *Sea Change* etc Dent
Joy Adamson *Born Free* Collins
Enid Bagnold *National Velvet* Heinemann
John Buchan *The Four Adventures of Richard Hannay* etc Hodder and Stoughton
Sheila Burnford *The Incredible Journey* Hodder and Stoughton
Nan Chauncy *The Roaring 40* etc OUP
Joyce Cary *Mr Johnson* etc Michael Joseph
Agatha Christie *Ten Little Niggers* etc Fontana
Jim Corbett *The Man Eaters of Kumaon* etc Penguin
Meindert De Jong *Far Out The Long Canal* etc Lutterworth

THE HOCKEY FIELD

Secondary school students receiving hockey instruction as a group.
The girls will then practise the new skill individually or in pairs

All children should be taught survival swimming. Here a junior boy
shows how trousers held between the knees can act as a buoyancy bag

TEACHERS WORLD

Fielding practice can take place indoors if necessary. The technique for catching a high ball is being demonstrated

Sir Arthur Conan Doyle *Sherlock Holmes* etc Murray
L. H. Evers *The Racketty Street Gang* Hodder and Stoughton
Rowena Farre *Seal Morning* Hutchinson
Elizabeth Gray *The Cheerful Heart* Macmillan
Ernest Gann *The Trouble With Lazy Ethel* etc Hodder and Stoughton
William Golding *Lord of the Flies* Faber
Ernest Hemingway *The Old Man and the Sea* etc Cape
Geoffrey Household *Rogue Male* etc Penguin
C. Walter Hodges *The Namesake* etc Bell
Cynthia Harnett *The Woolpack* etc Methuen
Hammond Innes *The Wreck of the Mary Deare* etc Collins
Geoffrey Jenkins *A Grue of Ice* etc Collins
Rudyard Kipling *Kim* etc Macmillan
John Masters *Night Runners of Bengal* etc Joseph
J. D. Salinger *The Catcher in the Rye* Penguin
Jack Schaefer *Shane* etc Corgi
Nevil Shute *No Highway* etc Heinemann
J. R. Tolkien *The Lord of the Rings* Allen and Unwin
Alison Uttley *A Traveller in Time* etc Faber
John Wyndham *The Kraken Wakes* etc Faber

Poetry
John Betjeman *A Ring of Bells* John Murray
E. Blishen *Oxford Book of Poetry for Children* OUP
Walter de la Mare *Come Hither* Faber
The Puffin Book of Verse Penguin
Edward Lear *Complete Nonsense* Faber
Ruth Manning-Saunders *A Bundle of Ballads* OUP
Herbert Read *This Way Delight* Faber
J. A. Smith *The Faber Book of Children's Verse* Faber

References
1 Lionel McColvin *Libraries for Children* Phoenix House 1961
2 Eleanor Graham writing in *Junior Bookshelf* November/December 1950
3 Ernest Roe *Teachers, Librarians and Children* Lockwood 1965
4 Ruth Viguers *Margin for Surprise: About Books, Children and Libraries* Constable 1966
5 Dorothy Neal *About Books for Children* OUP 1949
6 Eric Leyland *Libraries in Schools* Oldbourne 1961
7 Mary Atkinson *Junior School Community* Longmans 1949
8 Frank Whitehead *The Disappearing Dais* Chatto and Windus 1966

9 W. D. Wall *The Adolescent Child* Methuen 1948
10 See note 6 above
11 R. W. Purton writing in *Teachers World* 29th September 1967
12 N. M. Butterworth writing in *Teachers World* 8th March 1968
13 *Report on Education No 54: Public Libraries and Education* Department of Education and Science 1967

Further reading
Barbara Kyle *Teach Yourself Librarianship* EUP 1964
R. W. Purton *Surrounded by Books: The Library in the Primary School* Ward Lock Educational 1962
C. A. Stott *School Libraries: A Short Manual* CUP 1955

2

Sports and games

Most teachers will have received as part of their college course some basic training in the correct use of the physical education syllabus and instruction on taking physical education periods. Once they start working in schools there will be local advisers and organizers to run courses and provide individual assistance where it is needed. When it comes to sports and games however it will be found that these feature mainly as an out of school activity and that the teacher responsible for them has to find his own salvation.

Most boys and many girls are extremely keen on games and rely on teachers to provide coaching and organization. Obviously the extent to which teachers will engage in organized sport with the children as a spare time activity depends upon the enthusiasm with which they regard games. Some very good teachers actively detest games and with the best will in the world cannot but regard them as a chore to be carried out by the younger or more amiable members of the staff while others derive the utmost enjoyment from taking games as an out of school activity. An outstanding example of the latter was a male colleague with whom I shared digs in Twickenham. This young man seemed to throw his heart and soul into coaching the football, cricket and athletics every evening and most weekends. Came the first day of the summer holidays and I answered a knock at the door to find a group of children from the school clutching cricket equipment and asking anxiously if Sir was coming out to play!

The majority of teachers will be neither rabid exponents of sport nor confirmed haters of it, but merely conscientious men and women who realize that although they do not know a great deal about games their children will suffer unless they, the teachers, learn enough about the basics to be able to organize sport as a spare time activity. It is hoped that this chapter will provide enough material to enable any teacher to play a part in running sports and games at his or her school. A number of good fundamental books which may be recommended are noted at the end of the chapter.

The dimensions of pitches given in the text and on the diagrams are the metric equivalent of the present imperial measurements. The

Central Council of Physical Education will be publishing a leaflet giving precise details of metric measurements in early 1970.

In addition to reading about the organization of sports and games the teacher who wants to learn more about their operation and the latest coaching methods may attend various holiday courses run by the different coaching bodies. Two of the biggest are the Easter School of Physical Education held at Blackpool each year and the Loughborough College Summer School which provides instruction and the chance to gain practical experience in all manner of sports and pastimes. The Central Council of Physical Recreation organizes holiday courses throughout the country as do various national sporting bodies and many local education authorities. Details may be found in advertisements in the educational press.

Games in the infant school
Encouraging and assisting children to develop athletic and sporting skills through playing games may begin at an early age, certainly in the infant school. Very young children may not possess the competitive spirit which comes later and their muscular control and coordination will not be highly developed but most of them love to play games and this enthusiasm can be used to induce and foster various basic skills.

As with all infant work the games teacher will need patience and understanding. Few young children are able to concentrate for long periods but they are keen to learn and use new skills. As Julie Sharpe says in *PE Teachers' Handbook for Infant Schools*: 'If it is planned carefully with progressions according to the ability of the particular class, the children can enjoy the lesson at the same time as they are developing skills.'[1]

If possible the children should not be given the impression that they are being taught skills or anything else. They should be introduced to free play via the various games suggested at the end of this chapter and if they realize that in order to be more successful at the games they must learn how to throw better, run and jump more efficiently, handle apparatus etc then so much the better. The teacher should be on hand to demonstrate and offer advice but the development of skills should not be rushed as individual children will progress at different speeds.

While they are acquiring these skills and enjoying their games the infants will also be developing other abilities. They will be learning to think quickly, understand such things as fair play and the use of rules, improving their health and physique and widening their horizons.

The teacher should not expect too much too soon. Ivy Munden points out that infant children are not ready for some developments when she writes in *Physical Education for Infants*: 'Team work will be little used in infants' schools, but there is scope for working with a partner and cooperating in small groups with the older infants.'[2]

There are many different games which may be adapted for the infant school and some of them are developed and expanded later in the chapter. From simple singing and chasing games the children should move on to games involving the use of apparatus, thus laying the foundation for the organized games they will be playing in the primary and secondary schools. The games should encourage as much activity as possible, include all the children, be enjoyable for their own sake and involve the use of such pieces of apparatus as balls, bats, bean bags, skittles and rubber rings.

It goes without saying that the teacher should try to make the games as interesting and enjoyable as possible. At first the games could be a part of the physical education lesson but later separate games periods could be held, perhaps after school if the children are not too tired and the mothers of those engaged are willing to wait until the games are over before taking their children home. The games should be made progressively more difficult i.e. the children should have to run a little faster, coordinate more skills, throw a little farther, etc as they become more proficient. They should be encouraged to throw overarm as well as underarm and good style should always be encouraged when apparatus is used. No games are played standing still so the children should be encouraged to move about while bouncing balls, bowling hoops and so on.

Games in the primary school

In the primary school children may be introduced to organized individual and team games. To many teachers this means introducing the major sports like football and cricket, and while these are very popular with most children there are still many who are not ready for them. For those boys and girls who are not attracted to the hurly burly of competitive team sports the attractions of the minor games mentioned at the end of this chapter may prove stronger. Certainly in some schools less competitive sports and games are preferred until the children are at least nine.

The teacher who takes games as an out of school activity will have an advantage in that the pupils who wish to take part are all volunteers and are genuinely eager to play football, netball, hockey etc. This means that as a general rule the problem of dealing with children who are not interested does not arise, although it should be remembered that the basic ability of children will vary and that some very keen boys and girls may well have little coordination when it comes to playing games.

The teacher should decide from the start that if he is going to spend his spare time taking games with the children then it will be done properly. The children should not just be divided up into teams and allowed to get on with it. They must be taught the basic skills that will enable them to appreciate the relevant game to the full and get the most from it. Skills – dribbling, passing, throwing etc – should be taught individually as the need arises for them to be absorbed and then restored to the context of the game. As the games are being played the teacher should watch carefully and decide which individual skill needs demonstrating next. There is one drawback to this as Joseph Edmundson points out in *PE Teachers' Handbook for Primary Schools*.

> The recognized modern method of coaching or teaching any game or athletics event is to break it down to a series of fundamental or basic skills, practise these skills and from them rebuild the complete activity. In essence this is excellent theory and practice, but it is a method of teaching open to considerable abuse if carried to extremes.[3]

As Mr Edmundson says, skills should not be taught for their own sake. The children should enjoy the games they are playing and not have to stop playing them every five minutes to learn some trivial amendment or refinement.

Those children who are really keen on games will want to improve their standard and special coaching sessions could be arranged but even here the practices should be short and fairly frequent rather than long and drawn out.

With juniors care should be taken not to extend them too much physically. Playing pitches should be scaled down, nine year olds, for example, should not be allowed to play on a full size association football pitch. In many primary schools, of course, access to playing fields of any sort will be limited and most games will have to take place in the playground. As long as allowances are made for the hard surface and unusual angles and provided the children are not allowed to come into physical contact with each other they will be able to enjoy their games in the playground – but try to keep the children as far away from windows as possible.

The element of competition in sport when applied to young children worries some headteachers since they do not feel it right that too much emphasis should be placed on winning. To this end some heads even forbid school teams to enter local leagues and play against other school teams. At first this might seem an imposition both on the teacher willing to take games in his or her spare time and on the children denied the fruits of their practice and training, yet anyone who has seen a bad inter school league match at the primary level, with both teachers and parents shouting violently at the players and tending to lose their sense of proportion, will admit that there is something in the noncompetition theory. It should also be pointed out that if a teacher is devoting most of his or her spare time to coaching one school team, the other children who are not good enough for the team are missing out. Perhaps the ideal arrangement is to play the occasional friendly game against other schools and to concentrate more on inter house tournaments within the school. This is certainly a matter the young games teacher should discuss with the headteacher.

Games in the secondary school

Most if not all secondary schools will have physical education specialists on the staff and they will usually be responsible for the major organized sports if nothing else, but there is still plenty of scope for the non-specialist teacher to assist with games as an out of school activity. The physical education staff will usually welcome assistance and at the senior level there is a great demand for adults to help children with less usual sports. Many children who are reluctant to play football or hockey will develop an interest in sport if they are allowed to take up such things as badminton, table tennis, fencing, archery etc and volunteers from the staff to help coach such sports will as a rule be very welcome.

Coaching and organization

It would be impossible in the space available to give detailed coaching instructions for all the major sports and games but there are plenty of books available on this subject, including the ubiquitous *Know the Game* series. I hope in this chapter to give the nonspecialist a working outline knowledge of as many games and sports as possible, together with coaching hints and suggestions on organizing meetings and tournaments.

Athletics

The annual sports day or athletics meeting features as an important item on the calendar of most primary and secondary schools. At the majority of schools the coaching for the various events and the organization of the tournament will be out of school activities on the part of keen members of the staff.

The events making up the sports meeting will vary according to the age and ability of the children taking part. At the primary level, for example, no child should be allowed to run more than 100 metres in my opinion, although in a large senior school all the customary events may be included in the tournament.

On the actual sports day probably only the individual stars will be performing but the teachers responsible should see that in the preliminary heats every boy or girl wishing to take part should have had an opportunity to do so.

A satisfactory way of doing this is to arrange the athletics meeting on an inter house basis. Long before the final day every fit boy and girl in the school should be given an opportunity of representing his or her house. This can best be done by instituting a series of standard tests for the various age groups. Usually in a large school each child is requested to take part in three events – the high jump, the long jump and a running event, usually the 100 metres sprint. If there are plenty of willing teachers available to assist with the judging and the school has access to a playing field then more standard tests can be added, but three will be found to be enough under most circumstances.

For each of the three events a standard or qualifying level should be laid down. It is difficult to give examples as conditions and circumstances change from area to area and in a school with an athletics tradition and plenty of coaching facilities the overall standards will be higher than those in a school which has no such facilities. The best way to determine a satisfactory standard level will be for a teacher to take a dozen children of the same age and let them take part in the various jumps and sprints. As a result of their performances a good average may be arrived at which will become the standard to be reached. This should be repeated at all age levels in the school.

When the events and standards have been agreed upon they should be displayed on a large notice so that all the children are in no doubt as to what is expected of them. Then in games periods and after school all the children can try to reach the standards set in the three basic events. For each standard a boy or girl reaches (and there will of course be different standards for boys and girls of the same age) the child will receive one point to go towards the house total. Thus a good all rounder could gain a maximum of three points. This means that the final house placings will not depend upon the efforts of a few outstanding athletes on sports day but that every boy and girl in the school will have had a chance to contribute.

It will save time if the various events held to award standard points are also used as heats to select the finalists to compete on sports day. The finalists will have the chance of competing for more house points over and above those already received for passing their standard tests.

Children of secondary school age may want to spend some of their spare time training for the various athletics events but primary children are a little young for much training. Both ages, however, will benefit from coaching and some basic suggestions for different events may be found below.

Sprints
All children should be taught the correct start which is generally accepted to be the crouch start. The starter's commands will be 'on your marks' 'get set' or 'set' and then the starting pistol will be fired. The children should be taught how to approach the starting line and how to get away properly. The correct sequence is as follows:

1 The children stand about 3 m behind the starting line of the sprint.
2 The starter calls 'on your marks'.
3 The children approach the starting line and get into position for the crouch start as follows: the runner crouches with the front foot some 150–300 mm behind the line. The knee of the rear leg is placed beside the instep of the front foot. The arms are shoulder width apart with the hands, palm inward, resting just behind the starting line and the finger and thumb forming a bridge or arc. The body should be relaxed.
4 The starter calls 'get set' or 'set'.
5 The children raise their knees and push their shoulders forward slightly. The legs should not be completely straight yet. The body is held tense.
6 The starter fires the pistol or shouts 'go'.
7 The children push off strongly, driving forward and using short, fast strides. The rear foot is used to provide the impetus for the start. As the children run their bodies should gradually rise to the sprinting position.
8 The children sprint hard for the finishing line which is marked by a worsted tape.

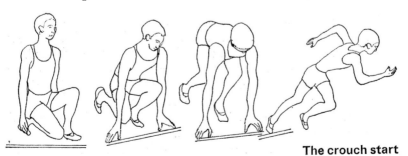

The crouch start

During coaching periods the teacher should demonstrate the crouch start to the children, pointing out that if it is used correctly it will give them a considerable advantage over competitors using a standing start. There are a number of practice exercises which can be used to good effect here. First of all the children can practise the start individually by just getting into position while the teacher walks round to make sure they have got the idea. Then the children can be divided into groups of six at a time. Each group will come up to the starting line, practise the crouch start and run on for about 10 metres.

A good way of discovering which children are using the crouch start to good advantage is to hold a series of races over 30 m. The children starting properly will have an advantage over naturally faster runners who have not yet mastered the crouch start.

The long jump
There are a number of techniques which can be applied to the long jump but those children with a real interest and ability in the event will be able to specialize in one of them when they become more proficient. I have always found that the simplest and most effective method to teach beginners is the sail style.

Most teachers will be familiar with the composition of a long jump pit. The children run along an approach and take off from the take off board or a line marked across the approach. They land in a pit filled with sand and providing they jumped off before they reached the line, they have completed the jump. The jump is measured from the take off line to the first mark made by the jumper in the sand, so if the jumper has fallen backwards his jump will be measured from the mark he made when he fell back.

This is the sequence for the sail style of long jump:
1 The child is told that it is his turn to jump.
2 He walks down to the take off line and measures back thirteen paces. He makes a mark after the thirteenth pace. This will be the spot from which he begins his run.
3 He is given the signal to start his jump.
4 He starts off on his take off foot i.e. his 'strong' foot and runs as hard as he can down the approach towards the line or take off board.
5 He reaches the take off board or line and jumps, placing his stronger foot on the board or line. If he goes over the line before jumping it will be a no jump and this will be called out.
6 He 'sails' through the air. As he jumps he bends his knees up to his chest and stretches his arms forward.
7 He comes down to land. Before landing in the pit he straightens his

legs and throws his arms back. Landing on his heels he then throws himself forward as hard as possible.

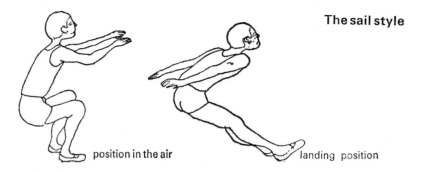

The sail style

position in the air   landing position

There are a number of ways in which the children can practise the sail style, although if possible such practice should be carried out using an actual long jump pit with its cushion of sand. The main thing to impress upon the children is that they must jump *high* if they are to jump long. One way of practising this is to suspend something in the air and as the children practise the take off and jump, concentrating on height rather than length, they have to reach up and touch the suspended article.

It should be emphasized that no high jump or long jump should be attempted unless there is a landing pit available full of sand, sawdust or some similar substance.

The high jump

There are a number of methods of achieving a good height in the high jump event but as with the long jump, the more sophisticated styles can be developed later. For beginners there are three basic styles to be demonstrated: the scissors, the straddle and the western roll. In the first of these, the scissors, the action sequence is as follows:

1 The child measures out a run up of seven paces.
2 The child starts his run at an angle of 45 degrees. He starts his run up on the foot which he will take off from.
3 After the seventh step he takes off on his jumping foot.
4 He swings up his leg nearest the bar.
5 He lifts both arms.
6 He lifts his other leg.
7 The first leg goes over the bar followed by the second leg in a scissors movement. Thus for a moment the child is almost in a sitting position over the bar.

8 He lands on the leg from which he took off.
9 He lowers his other leg to the ground.
   The scissors is a very basic style but it will give the child confidence and may be followed by coaching and practice in the straddle.
   The sequence for the straddle is:
1 The child measures a run up of seven paces.
2 He approaches the bar from an angle.
3 He plants his take off foot firmly beneath the bar.
4 He kicks his outside leg up and over the bar,.
5 He twists in the air so that he goes over the bar face downwards.
6 He twists his head and shoulders until they are on the far side of the bar with his knees bent and on either side of the bar.
7 His head and shoulders go down. He straightens and kicks upwards and backwards with his rear leg, thus clearing the bar with it.
8 He lands on the leg that cleared the bar first and both hands at the same time.
9 He rolls away from the bar.

The straddle

   The most advanced of the three relatively basic styles to be taught to high jump beginners is the western roll. The sequence is as follows:
1 The child measures out a run up of seven paces.
2 He starts on his jumping foot and approaches the bar at an angle.
3 He plants his jumping foot firmly on the ground.
4 He leans back slightly, kicks high with his outside foot and throws up his arms.
5 He twists so that he clears the bar with his body parallel to it.
6 His jumping leg is beneath his body and his other leg is almost straight.
7 He turns in the air to face the ground, reaching down with his hands and inside leg.
8 He lands on the inside leg and both hands and rolls away from the bar.

The western roll

All the styles described above can be practised over a bar only a few millimetres from the ground, but if the bar is raised then the jumps should only take place when a landing pit is available.

Hurdles

The various hurdles events are more suitable for senior than primary students although I have seen low hurdle races practised among younger children with some success. Any coaching in this event should concentrate on the basic style needed to clear the hurdles. This can be taught in the following sequence:

1 The child approaches the hurdle. His body leans forward and both arms go forward. His leading leg begins to straighten.
2 His body dips forward. His leading leg straightens over the hurdle. His other leg bends and lifts sideways from the hips.
3 His leading leg bends ready to be pushed down to the ground. His other leg is still being lifted sideways.
4 His leading leg reaches down to the ground. His trailing leg is now horizontal over the hurdle.

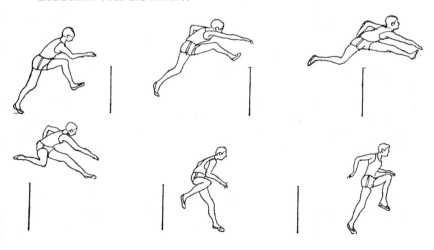

5 The arm over the trailing leg is pushed sideways and back.
6 The trailing leg is brought through sideways and forward ready for the next stride.
7 The child sprints for the next hurdle.

During practice it should be impressed on the child that only enough effort to clear the hurdle is necessary. It wastes time and energy to clear it by an unnecessary margin.

Relay races

The relay race is always popular with children and in an inter house competition this final team race can be very exciting. The two basic skills to be learnt here are the proper use of the changeover zone and handing on the baton.

The most popular of relays is the 4×110 metres race which is suitable for juniors as well as seniors. The first boys in each team are stationed on the starting line and the other three boys in each team are situated at intervals of 110 metres. At each changeover spot a 'box' 22 metres in length is drawn and the baton may be handed over anywhere within this changeover box. Should the baton be exchanged outside the box the team responsible will be disqualified.

For any relay race of this nature there is a staggered start and team members must stay in the lane allocated their team. The children should be taught that the responsibility for handing over the baton lies with the runner completing his leg of the race. The person who is receiving the baton begins to run as the other competitor approaches the changeover box, which extends for eleven metres on either side of the starting line, and must not look back or he will lose speed. The runner handing over the baton must place it down and across the outstretched hand of the other runner. The runner who is receiving the baton should be reaching back with the palm uppermost and thumb away from the fingers. His fingers close round the baton as he takes it over.

There are a number of other events, especially field events, which require tuition in basic skills, but if a teacher can coach his pupils in jumping and hurdling techniques, train them to start correctly in the sprints and hand over properly in the relay races then they will know enough to compete in an athletics tournament with both success and enjoyment.

Organizing a school athletics meeting

Any teacher or teachers who are willing to help organize the school athletics tournament must be prepared to put in a good deal of spare time if the tournament is to be successful. If the following details are attended to things should go fairly smoothly. It will help if the teachers concerned make a number of headings and tick them off as they have been arranged.

Date and time of meeting This will usually be decided by the headmaster or discussed at a staff meeting. A committee of interested teachers could be formed to organize things but one teacher should be in overall command to avoid confusion. This organizer can then delegate tasks to other helpers and be responsible for coordination.

The average sports meeting will be held in the summer months, usually at the end of term. It will help if the meeting is held early in the week so that if it has to be postponed due to bad weather it can be switched to later in the same week. If it is necessary to book the field on which the tournament is to be held it is advisable to pencil in another date for the same week in case of postponement.

It goes without saying that the date chosen should not clash with any other important school or external activity. The date should be announced as soon as it has been confirmed so that those children who care to can start training. At least two months notice should be given to allow housemasters etc to arrange the preliminary heats and standard tests.

Deciding upon events As soon as it has been decided to hold a sports meeting the committee should decide which events will be included. Later, when it comes to making up the programme, care must be taken to see that children competing in different events have a chance to rest between races and jumps, but in the initial stages a discussion of which races and jumps to include should be sufficient.

The sports field Some schools will have their own field and be able to lay out their own track while others will have to depend upon the services of a municipal or communal ground. If this is the case there is little that can be done in the way of basic alterations but for those teachers able to have some say in the layout of the field the following points could be borne in mind.

The running track should be the standard one i.e. circular and 440 m in diameter. At the primary level a straight 100 m track is sufficient. If a circular track is used races are run anticlockwise.

The long jump and high jump pits should be well away from the running track but situated so that the spectators can see what is going on. For the long jump pit the minimum recommended dimensions are: 6 m long, $1\frac{1}{2}$ m wide, 600 mm deep. The take off board should be painted white and about 1·2 m wide, fixed into the ground and level with the surface.

Preliminary activities If several months notice has been given there will be time to organize coaching, training and the preliminary heats.

Apparatus The following pieces of apparatus will be needed:

1 First aid kit and if possible a first aid hut or tent.
2 Megaphone for announcer, potatoes, eggs, etc for novelty races.
3 Ropes to keep back spectators, coloured bands for house teams.
4 Stop watches, batons, whistle for summoning athletes.
5 Seats for spectators, chair and table for recorder.
6 Large notice boards or blackboards, pistol and blank cartridges.
7 Record player and speakers for relaying music.
8 Numbers to be pinned onto competitors.
9 Steel measure, rake for long jump pit, plan of the course for officials.
10 Prizes – prominently displayed.
11 Finishing tape, judges' recording slips, starting and finishing posts.
12 Hurdles, high jump stands and bar, pegs for measuring throws.
13 Flags for relay judges.

Officials The following officials should be appointed and briefed well in advance:

1 Referee: to sort out any disputes (which should be kept to a minimum).
2 Timekeepers: three if possible so that the first three competitors in any event can be timed.
3 Starter: someone not afraid of firearms or loud noises and who possesses a penetrating voice.
4 Clerk of the course: sometimes known to his colleagues as muggins. It is his job to see that the course is laid out, equipment available, officials in the right place and so on.
5 Announcer: complete with monitors bringing results etc from the events.
6 Recorder: complete with results sheet already outlined.
7 Judges, programme sellers, stewards, someone to present prizes.

Miscellaneous If possible programmes should be provided even if they are only duplicated sheets. Competitors should all be neatly turned out in shorts and gym shoes. If refreshments are to be provided it is best to offer them at the end of the tournament rather than half way through it. No sports meeting should last more than three hours so do not include too many events. Working parties should be detailed to collect and return all equipment, clean up the field etc. Letters of thanks should be sent to any outsiders who helped.

Association football

As this is one of the major national games most boys are interested in soccer and there will be no shortage of volunteers to form teams in

Junior boys obviously enjoying their mime session

TEACHERS WORLD

Scottish children have constructed their own papier mâché puppets and theatre to illustrate the story of Bonnie Prince Charlie

schools. The inexperienced teacher taking on responsibility for organizing and coaching soccer should first make himself familiar with the layout of a soccer pitch. The size of the pitch will vary according to the age of the children playing but young children should never be asked to play on a full size senior pitch.

An association football pitch

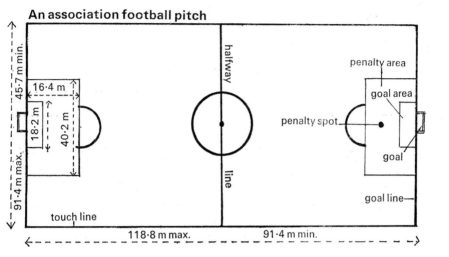

When it comes to coaching children, especially juniors, it will be found, as pointed out in *Planning the Programme* (HMSO) that:

> The outstanding problem is helping the players to keep in their places rather than to follow the ball about the field in a herd. This is a special difficulty when a heavy ball is used on a large pitch so that the players have not sufficient strength to make the ball move about freely. It is best to start from simple kicking games and to progress slowly to seven a side play on small pitches.[4]

The children will also have to be taught the positions in the game. Today with constantly changing techniques and patterns, the 3 – 4 – 3 formation, the 4 – 3 – 3 and other permutations, this can be confusing especially as the keener children may be more knowledgable and up to date than the teacher and be able to talk loftily of the centre back and deep lying centre forward and all the other terms beloved of sports writers. The teacher should resist the temptation to be drawn into such esoteric matters, at least until the children have a basic grasp of the normal positions.

If the incipient Bobby Charltons can be restrained, at least for the

		outside left	outside right		
left back	left half back			right half back	right back
		inside left	inside right		
goalkeeper	centre half back	centre forward	centre forward	centre half back	goalkeeper
		inside right	inside left		
right back	right half back			left half back	left back
		outside right	outside left		

time being, the children should be taught the basic functions of each position – the goalkeeper and full backs to defend, the half backs to forage, supporting their forwards and going back in defence, and the forwards to attack. This can all be explained in theory before the boys actually go onto a pitch and then they can be allowed to play a game almost at once in order to maintain their enthusiasm. Later on the various skills involved should be explained and demonstrated as the need to use them arises. These fundamentals can be divided into five basic skills.

Dribbling The boys should be taught how to walk and then run maintaining full control over the ball at their feet. The best way to develop this skill is to let the boys get the feel of the ball individually by walking with it between their feet, pushing the ball from one foot to another, always keeping the ball close to the foot. They can then move on to pushing the ball alternately with the inside and outside of first one foot then the other. Finally a combination of these movements should be used, still at a walking pace. When some measure of dexterity has been achieved the boys can go on to doing the same things when running and then dribbling the balls round obstacles. Team relay races can be used to bring an element of competition to the practice.

Kicking The boys should first be taught to kick low and straight. The sequence for this is to approach the ball from an oblique angle, placing the non kicking foot squarely by the side of the ball. The knee and head should be over the ball when the kicking foot swings through with the toe firmly under the ball so that it is kicked with the part of the boot covered by the laces. The leg swings from the hip and carries through after the shot with the toe pointing towards the target.

Practice for this can include kicking the ball from boy to boy and kicking at targets.

Defenders should also master the high clearance kick. The sequence for this shot is to place the non kicking foot to the rear and one side of the ball, lean the body to one side and follow right through with the kicking foot.

Passing In order to pass a ball accurately a player should dribble the ball towards the target and then, when he is sure a fellow player is in position, use the inside of his foot to pass the ball with the toe turned at right angles to the direction of passing; the foot should follow through pointing towards the target. Boys can practise this move in pairs, using both feet alternately.

Trapping If the ball bounces near a player he should trap it by placing his foot over the ball and forcing it down thus deadening the bounce. Almost at once the ball should be pushed forward and a dribble, kick or pass initiated.

The trainer can lob high balls to all the boys in turn to give them a chance to practise this skill.

Heading If a ball is to be headed the player must learn to keep his whole attention on it as it comes through the air. The player meets the ball with his forehead, jumping if need be to outdistance another player and then nods it in the requisite direction. The impetus should come from the player, not the ball.

The teacher responsible for football should take care that the balls used are looked after, stored properly and kept in good condition. The manufacturers should supply the correct attachment for inflating the balls and this only should be used. Do not dry the ball in front of a fire but wipe the mud and water off with a cloth and then allow it to dry naturally. The ball should never be inflated to its full capacity. At the end of the season all footballs should be deflated and not inflated again until the beginning of the next season.

Hockey

As with football any teacher intending to supervise hockey in a school or as an out of school activity should first make herself acquainted with the layout of the hockey pitch and the names and functions of the various positions.

The positions in hockey tally to a great extent with those of the soccer team and the basic functions are also much the same. The defence is in the hands of the goalkeeper and the right and left backs. The goalkeeper is allowed to kick the ball in defence of her goal; it is essential when filling this position to select a girl of steady temperament and cool judgement. The two backs mark the opposite inners and should be able to feed their own forwards.

A hockey pitch

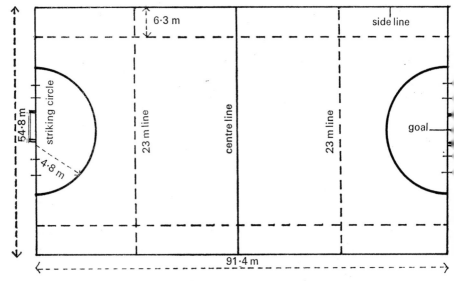

The half backs are also responsible for marking the opposing forwards. The left half back should check the opposing right wing, the centre half back marks the centre forward of the opposing team and the right half back marks the opposite left wing. As in soccer the half backs have to support their own forwards in attack yet always be in a position to come back in defence.

The forwards – right wing, right inner, centre forward, left inner and left wing – should concentrate on scoring goals, keep in line with their centre forward and be ready to snap up any chances to score. The players on the wing should try to make as much ground as possible before passing to their forwards in the centre.

The children should be given as many opportunities as possible to practise using hockey sticks as well as mastering skills such as bullying off, dribbling, passing etc. The players should be taught not to be selfish on the field and to stick to their positions. Playing with one hand should be discouraged as both accuracy and control will be lost unless both hands are used. The players should be encouraged to pass straight away and not to hold on to the ball and thus give opponents a chance to get back into position.

	left wing		right wing	
left back	left half back	left inner	right inner	right half back	right back
goalkeeper	centre half back	centre forward	centre forward	centre half back	goalkeeper
right back	right half back	right inner	left inner	left half back	left back
	right wing		left wing	

Hockey positions

Wing forwards must always stay in position even if they are being starved of the ball. All things being equal it is usually better to centre at the 23 m line, but if the opportunity presents itself the pass may be delayed even as far as the goal line. When the winger does centre the ball should be allowed to drop slightly behind the player. As the wingers are usually closely marked they should vary their play as much as possible.

Inners should take care to avoid crowding their centre forward, learn to shoot at every opportunity and build up a good understanding with their wing partners.

The centre forward spot should be reserved for the most forceful and versatile player in the team, someone who can shoot, dribble and move at high speed and possesses a good tactical sense. The best formation to use among inexperienced players is one which has the centre forward flanked by the inners.

The half backs must be resolute tacklers and players with a great deal of determination, able to mark their opposite numbers carefully and constantly. The three halves must build up a good understanding and cover one another whenever possible. At the same time every opportunity must be taken to give the forwards possession of the ball.

The full backs should be calm and selfpossessed, able to trap the ball and distribute it accurately. They must also build up a good understanding with each other and cover each other. They must avoid wild hitting and dribble as little as possible near their own goal.

The goalkeeper should have a good sense of timing, quick reflexes and keen eyesight. She must learn the art of stopping the ball so that it does not rebound out of control.

When it comes to practice for hockey the players can work in pairs, passing to each other, dribbling and passing on the move, hitting the ball to each other, hitting from the shoulders while not raising the head of the stick above shoulder level and flicking the ball with a strong twist of the wrists.

The basic skills to be practised are:

Dribbling The stick should be held with the left hand at the top and the right hand half way down. The stick is kept as close to the ball as possible and inclined forward to keep the ball on the ground and used to push the ball along the ground.

Passing The usual grip applies here, with the stick placed against the ball. The ball is pushed forward but the stick maintains contact with it. The player then lunges forward with the left foot and the whole body is swung behind the ball pushing it away sharply in the required direction.

Trapping The usual grip is maintained. If the ball approaches at ground level the body should be manoeuvred so that the ball approaches from the right. The stick should be held upright or vertical. As the ball strikes the stick both wrists should yield. The ball should stop and the player can dribble or pass. If the ball approaches through the air the player should raise the stick with the flat surface towards the oncoming ball and the fingers of both hands facing the ball. The ball strikes the flat surface of the stick and is deflected downwards to the player's feet, ready for the next move.

Driving or shooting Both hands are held close together at the top of the stick. The left foot is held poised with the weight on the right foot. The stick should be swung back in line with the ball and then as the left foot steps forward the body surges towards the ball. The stick should hit the ball at the bottom of the swing. The player's eyes should be on the ball and there should be a controlled follow through.

Netball

This is one of the most popular of games with girls of all ages and there will be plenty of opportunities to introduce it as an out of school activity. The game does not require a playing field and has the advantage of being suitable for the school playground. The layout of a netball pitch and the positions of the players are as shown in the diagram.

Goal shooter As the name indicates it is the job of this player to try and

A netball court showing team positions at the start of a game

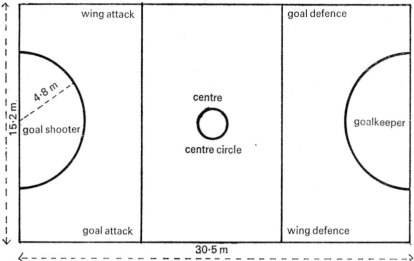

score from within the circle. It is a position for a selfconfident player who shoots accurately.

Goal attack This player feeds the goal shooter with as many passes as possible and is in position in the circle to collect any rebounds and try for shots herself.

Wing attack This player operating on the right hand side of the court or playing area, is responsible for receiving a steady flow of passes from the centre and passing them on to the goal shooter and attack.

Centre This player acts as a link in the team by obtaining the ball from the centre and redistributing it to the wing attack, the attack and occasionally the goal shooter.

Wing defence This player, operating on the left hand side of the court, should receive the ball from the defence and the goalkeeper and then pass it on to the centre. At the same time she should mark the opposing wing attack.

Goal defence This player is responsible for marking the opposing goal attack and is responsible, with the goalkeeper, for getting the ball out of the team's circle and out to the defending centre.

Goalkeeper It is the duty of the goalkeeper to mark the opposing goal shooter.

Netball coaching should include practice in the appropriate skills i.e. passing, shooting, dodging and marking. While individual practices will always help, much can be done within the scope of a normal game.

Cricket

Cricket is usually the most popular summer game among boys of all ages, and the first thing a prospective coach should do is to ensure that he knows the correct way to lay out a pitch and the names of all the fielding positions.

There are eleven men in a cricket team but the number of fielding positions into which they can be put is considerably higher than this. The positions are:

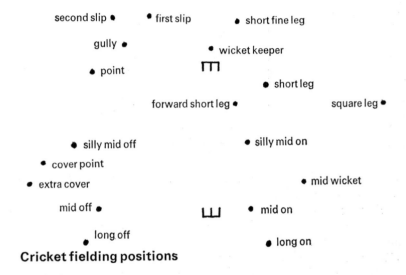

Cricket fielding positions

Although cricket purists will probably shudder at the thought, I have always found it advisable to include with young children the ubiquitous field placing of long stop immediately behind the wicket keeper. This placing should not be necessary with older boys however.

A full length cricket pitch should be 20 m in length. With juniors a distance of 17 m will usually be found to be sufficient. The actual measurements of a full size pitch are shown in the diagram.

The boys should be taught the basic batting stance and several of the more common strokes. The correct stance consists of the player standing with his feet about 150 mm apart and parallel. One foot should be on either side of the line known as the batting crease. The knees should be slightly bent and the weight distributed on the balls of both feet. The bat should be grasped by the handle with the right hand underneath the left and both hands just touching. The bat should be placed behind the toe of the right foot with the batsman looking over his left shoulder down the pitch at the bowler. In order to lift the bat back for a stroke most of the force should be exerted with the left hand. The elbows should be kept clear of the body.

The forward defensive stroke is played by lifting the bat back in the manner described above. Then the left foot is placed down the wicket to the left of the flight of the ball. The bat follows through face forward. The right foot should stay inside the batting crease and the left knee is bent and the bat inclined forward to make sure that the ball does not pop up. The bat should make contact with the ball near the batsman's left foot.

In order to drive the ball the usual backlift is used and then, with the bat still lifted, the batsman steps forward on the left foot. The right foot is then brought up to the left foot. The left foot goes forward to where the batsman expects the ball to bounce and the bat is swung down and forward in the line of the flight of the ball. The ball strikes the bat and the bat follows through.

Every opportunity should be given for the boys to practise these two strokes until they have mastered them. Plenty of fielding practice should be given and the natural bowlers selected for further coaching in flight speed and length.

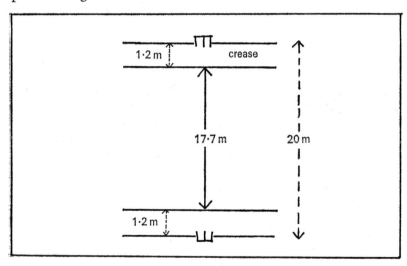

Swimming

In addition to being an enjoyable sport, swimming is an essential skill for every boy and girl. If there is a swimming pool near the school every opportunity both in and out of school hours should be taken to coach children in the basic strokes. The teacher should do more than coach children in swimming techniques because even experienced swimmers can drown through carelessness. All children should be warned about possible hazards and be taught how to apply artificial respiration in emergencies.

A considerable amount of preliminary practice can take place on land before the children are taken to a swimming pool. As Mabel Davies points out in *Physical Education, Games and Athletics*:

> Where the water work must be confined to the summer, swimming instruction should start early in the spring in the form of *land drill* which teaches the class the correct movements and timing of the breast stroke or crawl, so that when they reach the water the particular stroke can be done automatically and the child is not called upon to attempt new and difficult coordinated movement in such a strange and confusing medium as the water.[5]

As a rule the breast stroke is the first stroke taught to children and this lends itself to land drill. The arm stroke can be demonstrated and practised while the children are standing, and then the arm and leg strokes combined can be practised while the children are supported in a prone position. When both arm and leg positions have been mastered the children can move on to the shallow end of the swimming pool, and as ability and confidence improve to the deep end.

Many schools hold a swimming gala once a year and the same arrangements which precede an athletics tournament hold good, in outline, for a swimming gala. The individual events will depend upon the capabilities of the children taking part. In *Handbook for Sports Organizers* Joseph Edmundson recommends a selection from the following events as a programme for a secondary school gala:

1. One length breast stroke: under 12, 13, 14 and 15 years of age
2. Two lengths breast stroke (open)
3. One length free style (ages as above)
4. Two lengths free style (open)
5. One length back stroke (open)
6. Two lengths back stroke (open)
7. One length butterfly breast stroke (open)
8. One length butterfly dolphin stroke (if known by competitors)
9. Novices' breast stroke, crawl and back stroke competitions
10. Crawl, breast stroke, back stroke etc style competitions (open)
11. Firm or spring board diving competition
12. Inter house or team relay (free style)
13. Inter house or team medley relay
14. Invitation inter school relay or medley relay
15. Plunge (open)

16   Swimming or diving exhibitions by expert swimmers, life saving demonstrations or humorous events.

17   Short water polo match, either by the school team (if such exists) against another school or a match arranged through the cooperation of the local swimming club.

The actual conditions under which swimming should be taught have been described in *Planning the Programme*:

> The water should be clean and the bottom of the pool should be firm and not slippery. The children will need a rail, rope or pole by which to steady themselves and to give support for various practices. The depth of the water is important, for if a child is immersed much above his waistline his balance becomes precarious and his confidence is shaken. Some teachers prefer to teach in water which is so shallow that the children are able to lie prone and to touch the bottom with their hands without submerging their faces. A large area of water is likely to be more alarming to a beginner than a small pool and if children cannot be taught in a pool designed for beginners it may be necessary to make temporary barriers with poles or ropes in order to have a small enclosure for them. Nonswimmers are apt to become cold rather quickly and they do better in water which is kept at a higher temperature than would be usual for swimmers.[6]

The breast stroke Before attempting this stroke there should be plenty of land drill first. This should be followed at the baths by practice in coasting. This consists of standing hip deep in the water and then launching oneself forward into the water, arms extended beyond the head and floating face downwards to the side of the bath. This should be practised until the children can coast the best part of a width of the bath.

In order to learn the breast stroke the children should lie chest down in the water. Their arms should be extended in front of their heads with the palms touching and fingers closed. The legs should be held as straight as possible with the heels together. In order to make the arm stroke the palms should be turned outward and the arms swept downwards and backwards on a line with the shoulders. The hands should should be brought together under the chin and pushed forward. The legs should be brought up with the knees bent and spread and then kicked out and apart before being brought together again.

Diving When the children are confident enough to begin diving they should be shown the correct sequence. The hands should be held over the head with the thumbs together and the palms down. Then the child jumps off the board or side of the bath in a curving motion. The body should be straight when it enters the water, with the arms ahead to break the surface and the toes together behind.

Minor or miscellaneous games

These games can be used in their own right, adapted to suit the age of the children taking part or used as warming up activities before coaching and practice for the major sports.

Free tag One player is chosen to chase the others. If a player is touched he joins the first 'he' and helps him touch the others who try to escape. The game continues until only one player has not been caught.

Lifting race Two or more teams sit in a straight line with their legs extended before them. When the teacher shouts 'go' all the children extend their arms sideways. The last child in each team stands up, puts his hands under the arms of the child in front and lifts him. That child does the same thing to the child in front of him and so on. The winning team is the one with all its members standing up.

Cat and mice One child – the 'cat' – goes out in front of the rest of the class with his or her back to the rest. The others – the 'mice' – creep up on the cat. As soon as the cat hears them she turns and gives chase but if the cat turns and everyone is still, she may not chase the mice. Everyone caught in the chase becomes a cat.

Ankle pushing Two boys grip their own ankles and crouch opposite each other. Still holding their ankles they try and push each other over, using their shoulders.

Free and caught Two 'hunters' are chosen. The other children scatter. If a hunter touches a child he or she must 'freeze' but can be released by a touch from a free child.

Tunnel race Two or more teams stand in straight lines, feet apart, to form a tunnel. At the signal to start the last child in each team crawls through the legs of the others to the front and then stands up straight with feet apart. The last but one child does the same and so on until each member of the team has been through the tunnel.

Rabbits in the hole The class should be divided into teams of three. Numbers 1 and 2 in each team join hands to form the 'hole'. Number 3, the 'rabbit', stands between them. One child should be outside – he or she is the strange rabbit. At a signal all the rabbits have to change holes by running to another team and the odd rabbit out must try to get into one of the empty holes. The rabbit unable to get to a hole takes over as the strange rabbit.

Catch your partner The class is divided up into pairs. At a signal one partner runs away from the other and the other child tries to catch his or her partner. When the teacher signals a halt those partners who have not been caught have to change round and become the chaser.

Circle tag The children form up in a circle, facing in the same direction. At a signal they all start running in a circle, each child trying to touch the child in front. If a child is touched he drops out.

Knock out (boys only) The class is formed up into teams. Each team forms a circle with hands joined. One boy from another team tries to get into each circle by forcing his way in while the other team resists.

Dodge ball The children scatter. One child is given a ball and has to hit the other children with it. If a child is hit he or she has to help the thrower.

Double circle tag The class forms a double circle. Two children are picked and they chase each other in and out of the circle. If the child being chased stops in front of a pair in the circle, the back member of the pair has to take the place of the one being chased.

Pig in the middle The children divide into groups of three. Each group has one ball. One child goes in the middle of each group and the other two throw the ball to each other. The child in the middle tries to intercept the ball. If he does so, the last one to throw the ball takes his place in the middle.

Train tag The children form in groups of three. Two children form the 'train', one of them holding on to the hips of the one in front. The third child tries to join onto the train. When he or she is successful the leading child then takes his or her place and tries to join on in turn.

Threading the needle Each child stands holding his or her hands together in front. At a signal from the teacher the children attempt to place their legs through their clasped hands and back again.

Crusts and crumbs The children are divided into two teams, facing each other. One team is called crusts and the other crumbs. The teacher calls out one of these names. If crusts is called the crusts run away pursued by the crumbs. Any crust caught is out of the game.

Team dodge ball The class is divided up into three teams. Two teams stand on either side of the playground and the third team goes in the middle. The teams on either side throw a ball at the team in the middle, trying to hit the children below the knees. Each team goes into the middle for the same length of time. The winning side is the one with the fewest hits registered against it.

Chase the bag All the children scatter about the playground. Four of them are given bean bags. Two hunters are chosen who must try to touch a child in possession of a bag. The children in possession run and dodge or pass the bag to another child. Any child caught with a bag joins the hunters.

References

1 Julie M. Sharpe *PE Teachers' Handbook for Infant Schools* Evans 1959
2 Ivy Munden *Physical Education for Infants* OUP 1953
3 Joseph Edmundson *PE Teachers' Handbook for Primary Schools* Evans 1956
4 *Planning the Programme* HMSO 1953
5 Mabel Davies *Physical Education, Games and Athletics* Allen and Unwin 1959
6 See note 4 above

Further reading

Moving and Growing HMSO 1953
J. Edmundson *Handbook for Sports Organizers* Evans 1960
J. Edmundson *PE Teachers' Handbook for Secondary Schools* Evans 1957
Know the Game series (*Cricket, Association Football* etc) Educational Productions 1950/70
M. W. Randall and W. K. Waine *Objectives in Physical Education* Bell 1968
Eric Guillen *Safety Games and Exercises* Bell 1968

3

Drama, movement and speech

The most likely way in which a teacher will use his interest and knowledge of drama, movement and speech may well be in producing the
school play or concert but there are other out of school activities like
drama clubs, dances and debating societies where it will also be useful.

The teacher should differentiate between child drama and theatre.
R. N. Pemberton-Billing and J. D. Clegg explain the difference in
Teaching Drama:

> Child drama is not theatre. All too frequently drama in schools is
> a diluted version of adult theatre, conducted as if the aim were to
> train actors for the stage. Acting involves the use of techniques
> developed for the sole purpose of communicating with an audience,
> and requires the actor to bring to life ideas and conflicts for the
> benefit, not of himself, but of his audience. . . . This is not to say
> that theatre is either bad or wrong, but merely that it should not be
> confused with child drama. Theatre can be a useful and enjoyable
> out of school activity: child drama is an educational medium.[1]

If a teacher is really interested in drama and the theatre he can cater for
both by running a drama club in the evening which encourages and
follows the principles of group drama and creativity and, at the end of
the term, produce an orthodox school play using the children from the
drama club who have proved themselves to be willing and enthusiastic.
In its early days at any rate a drama club for children should be based
upon improvised play. As Richard Courtney says in *Teaching Drama*:

> In drama, children play. Improvised play is the basis of all drama
> teaching. The children create their own drama from hints and
> suggestions given by the teacher. But the drama, the children play-
> ing, is their own; it is their own imagination expressed. We may,
> as teachers, assist their dramas by ancillary work; where we cannot
> hear clearly what the actors say, for example, we may introduce
> speech work that will help them. But the child's creation comes
> first.[2]

Many children take eagerly to creative drama, especially when they have overcome any shyness or lack of selfconfidence. All children like playing, creating their own world and at times escaping from the real one yet also coming to terms with life by making up their own responses to it in their play.

In the drama club the children should be allowed to improvise their own situations. Later they can move on to scripted plays but at first they should not have to cope with other people's ideas and speech but rather bring their own personalities to the drama. Such dramatic play can begin early in life, indeed it can 'begin in the nursery as a means of creative activity, of imaginative play, of the use of powers of speech and movement to express more vividly the picture formed in the mind.'[3]

The teacher's part in such creativity should be unobtrusive but is extremely important. He or she should try and see the child's activities as the child sees them from within. In his different mimes and plays the child is not giving a picture of the world but of the world as he sees it and reacts to it. The teacher should not expect polished results; if the child is involved completely in what he is doing then he is getting something out of the experience.

This does not mean that the teacher's part is a passive one – far from it. In all activities there has to be organization and there has to be discipline. If a general free for all is allowed the extroverted children may have a fine time but the quieter ones may well be squashed in more than one sense. In *Group Drama* D. E. Adland writes: 'The keystone of any form of group work is that the teacher already has good class control – so that he can delegate some of his authority to the group without fear of chaos or slipshod work.'[4]

In the early stages of running a drama club as an out of school activity most of the work can be done as a class, especially during activities which involve the children performing and practising individually. Sooner or later, however, it will be found more practicable to divide the club up into more manageable groups. During the formative stages of the club's existence the teacher should attempt to assess the character and personality of the different children. Then when the time comes to split the class up into groups it should be possible to ensure that each group contains a cross section of noisy and quiet children, imaginative and slower children and so on. Avoid having more than eight in a group or the members will never come to any decisions or less than six in case crowd scenes are called for.

For some time the teacher can continue work involving the whole class even though groups have been formed. The evening's activities can begin with warming up mimes or exercises and then the children

A visit from the local fire service can be a lively introduction to an interesting career or provide material for project work

TEACHERS WORLD

School leavers interested in a nursing career pay a visit to the local hospital

can split into groups for their creative work. Another advantage of group work in drama is that it allows the teacher to keep in touch with the members by going from group to group with suggestions and encouragement. While he is with one group the others have time to plan and carry out their own activities without too much interference.

Many drama clubs will fall into their own routines without too much trouble but in the early stages the teacher might like to consider following a timetable something like this:

Assembling the children If the club is fairly small meetings could be held in a classroom, otherwise the school hall or gymnasium will have to be used.

Warm up activities These could include miming to suggestions from the teacher, or moving around the space available to the music of a record player. Anne Driver in *Music and Movement* describes the purpose of this activity:

> The first aim is to try and find the child's own natural rhythm unrelated to music or any dictates from the teacher. It must be fully realized that each child has his own individual rhythm, with its coefficients of movement, speed and character. Observation shows the great difference between the movements of the eager dynamic child and those of the lethargic or timid.[5]

Whether the children move to music or whether they merely spend the opening minutes miming and imitating, the teacher should still be in command of the situation. He or she could suggest to the children various ways of moving. This could take the form of commands: 'Pretend you're something at sea – a wave, a storm, a ship. . . . Now you're something in the air – a cloud, the sun . . . be a bird . . . be an animal . . . be a piece of machinery in a factory' and so on.

The teacher should make sure at this stage that every child is engrossed in what he or she is doing and is not being extended beyond his or her scope. For example if a child has never been near a factory it might be asking too much to expect him or her to mime the workings of a piece of factory machinery. If the suggested piece of mime is too trivial or absurd the child will think it beneath him and start playing around or showing off.

Group mime The children may be divided into groups and asked to mime certain crowd or group activities. In the early stages the teacher will give each group a choice of activities but later the groups may decide upon their own. It is not uncommon to find a certain piece of mime becoming a favourite with a particular group who will repeat it again and again. As long as the mime continues to grow and is not stereotyped there is nothing wrong with this and each group can be encouraged to polish its own party piece as long as plenty of fresh work is done each week.

The teacher can suggest situations for group mime such as a street accident, a football match, an orchestra and so on. Each group should be given plenty of time in which to practise its mimes and then it should play them out while the other groups watch.

Discussion of mime After each group has finished its mime the teacher should make comments and find out from the children just what they had set out to do. If possible encourage the children to criticize their own mime and those of the other groups as this will be a valuable exercise. Perhaps some of the children will think up better ways of performing a certain action or decide to alter various sequences; there are many things that might grow out of discussion and analysis. As with all subjects the teacher should not dominate the discussion but just set it going and keep it on the right tracks.

Individual speech practice Speech is just as important a part of drama as movement and the children must be given plenty of opportunities to improve and perfect their speech. Again the teacher can suggest certain exercises which will give the children confidence. Each child could be asked to pretend to be an announcer at a railway station, a man selling something in a market, a master of ceremonies at a boxing match etc. Later the children can be divided into pairs and given roles to perform – two friends meeting in the street, a sentry challenging a soldier, two housewives talking over a garden fence and so on.

Group speech practice After individual practice the groups can assemble to practise communal speech work. Again the teacher can provide situations for the children to develop – heckling at a meeting, cheering a football team, saying goodbye to friends at a railway station – and the children can develop them and also come up with their own ideas. Through being grouped they should also learn something about the art of social behaviour such as getting on with each other and all working towards a common goal.

Group practice in movement and speech When the children are sufficiently confident and experienced they can combine both movement and speech and improvise situations and short plays. These can be taken from life or from well known stories and poems.

Drama from scripts If the children seem particularly fond of a story they could tell it in their own words and turn their dialogue into a fairly sophisticated little play. When they have done this a number of times they will be ready to take part in scripted plays.

66

The school play

The school play, strictly speaking, comes under the heading of theatre rather than drama. Usually children are working from a prepared script and are voicing the sentiments of the character they portray rather than their own feelings. This need not always be the case however. It is possible for children to improvise their own drama in the various ways discussed above and yet still perform it before an audience as an orthodox scripted play.

This is done by allowing the children to improvise their own drama and then, once it has acquired a definite shape, to write down and learn the parts. In this way the parts in the play will bear some resemblance to the children portraying them because the characters will have sprung from the personalities of the children who created them.

I had some experience of a play of this sort with a drama club in a dock area primary school. There were some twenty children in the club representing all ability levels and aged between nine and eleven. The children had enjoyed the various forms of mime and speech training and after the club had been in existence for about a year I suggested that they might like to put on a Christmas play. This suggestion was made in September. The children were enthusiastic about the idea and we discussed what the play should be about. In previous years some of the fourth year classes had produced orthodox scripted nativity plays and the children in the club, with little experience of any other sort of drama, decided that they too would like to produce a nativity play.

Several ideas for the background and setting of the play were put forward by the children but were not greeted very warmly. After some discussion it was decided that the play ought to be about the birth of Jesus and that it should take place in the Holy Land at the time of the birth of Jesus.

At this point no more ideas were forthcoming and the meeting broke up with everyone promising to think about the matter and to come up with ideas at the next meeting of the drama club.

At the next meeting several of the older children put forward the idea of setting the play in the inn and the stable in which Jesus was born. They said that the cast could include Joseph and Mary, the innkeeper, the shepherds and the three kings.

The other children received this suggestion eagerly and would willingly have taken it up. At this point, however, I felt that it was time for the teacher to interfere. If the children were allowed to go ahead unrestrained all that would emerge would be a copy of all the other nativity plays they had seen. In order to prevent this I applauded the idea of setting the play in the inn but asked the children why Joseph and

Mary had been forced to sleep in the stable. The answer came at once that the inn had been full. I then asked them what sort of people would have been staying there. At this stage Philip, one of the fourth year members of the club, said with confidence that there would be all sorts – 'a right old collection'. He knew this because his father kept one of the local pubs.

This happy chance gave the play fresh impetus. The children began to identify the inn of the Bible story with the pub kept by Philip's father; it suddenly seemed to become much more real to them. They had all passed the public house at lunch time and in the evening and knew what a mixed collection of people went there.

I pointed out that the inn at Bethlehem would have been like that too. If we did a play about it we ought to people the inn with ordinary people who would have been staying there. We then thought about what sort of people might have been staying there and as the children realized that just about anybody could have been staying at the inn they began to talk about which characters they would like to be. I told them all to think about it and that at the next meeting we would begin to improvise scenes from our nativity play.

Over the next couple of months the play slowly took shape, although it was never the same two weeks running. The only thing that remained constant was the character adopted by each child. Some chose the orthodox biblical characters – the shepherds and the kings – but most evolved their own imaginative creations. Philip, perhaps naturally, became the innkeeper; Stanley, the class clown, became a drunk at the bar; another child became a commercial traveller (transformed as the children began to read and enquire about the period into a travelling carpet seller); a girl became a district nurse on her way to a confinement. There were parents and children, a soldier going home on leave, a couple of youths looking for a dance and so on.

As the children grew into their characters and began to improvise actions and dialogue I took care not to interfere except to give advice: What army would the soldier belong to? What sort of entertainments would the youths be looking for? What drinks and food would be served at the bar? The children rehearsed in groups in different corners of the public bar and then came together for crowd scenes. If something seemed particularly good I suggested that it be kept, if a scene was dull or pointless I asked the cast if they wanted to keep it in.

The children seemed to enjoy improvising and rehearsing the scenes but they felt that the play ought to have a climax. After some discussion they decided that the end would come with the shepherds arriving and telling them that the King of Kings had been born in the stable behind the inn. The guests would forget all their squabbles and problems and go out with the shepherds to worship Jesus.

This simple basic plot provided a framework within which the children could work out their relationships. As time went by, however, the plot took fresh twists and in the end the emphasis had changed completely. The first half of the play was occupied with the interplay of characters in the inn. Then the shepherds came to worship the new born Christ and convinced all the guests that he really was the Son of God. At the end of the play Roman soldiers entered the inn searching for any babies. The guests put aside their differences, refused bribes and paid no attention to threats. The Romans left and the guests, united for once, went out to worship Jesus in the stable.

This very simple plot was appreciated by the children and after some months when they had worked out a polished version, they wrote their own words and reactions to the situations in the play and used them for the final version which was performed on the stage in front of the rest of the school.

The advantage of this way of making plays lies in the fact that each child can find his own level. Those with plenty of confidence can assume large parts, others can be walk ons, but because each part is created entirely by the child playing it no one feels ignored or out of things.

Scripted plays

Creative drama and plays made up by the children involved in them have an important part to play in any dramatic work attempted in schools but this does not mean that orthodox scripted plays should not be rehearsed and performed. Such plays form an important part of the social life of the school, introduce both actors and audience to important and interesting forms of drama, encourage the children to discipline themselves into learning the fundamentals of acting, stage management, etc and show the children the need for an importance of teamwork.

There are many plays suitable for children of all ages and abilities. Teachers are advised to send off to the various publishers for reading copies of plays they think might be suitable. Some of the major publishers in this field are:

Deane, 31 Museum Street, London EC1
Evans, Montague House, Russell Square, London WC1
French, 26 Southampton Street, Strand, London WC2
League of Dramatists, 84 Drayton Gardens, London SW10
Radius Religious Drama Society, George Bell House, Ayres Street, London SE1

When it comes to selecting the right play for the cast the teacher will have to draw upon his or her knowledge of the children involved. With the right children and the right teacher there is no limit to the scope possible. A great deal of school drama is second and third rate but some is first rate and the best results are not always obtained by playing for safety in the choice of play. Anyone who has seen a reasonable amount of school drama will have seen excellent productions of many by Shakespeare, Ibsen and O'Neill as well as of more typical plays like *Tobias and the Angel* (Bridie), *The Ghost Train* (Ridley) and *Price of Coal* (Brighouse).

All the above plays of course could only be put on by senior boys and girls. There are some effective plays for juniors but as a rule only short scripted plays should be attempted by younger children and in my opinion no child under the age of nine should become too heavily involved with scripted plays.

Once the play has been selected and the date of production arranged the producer should make sure that he understands the play thoroughly. By repeated readings of the script he will come to understand exactly what the author is getting at, the personalities of the characters in the play, the rhythm of the various scenes – where the action should be speeded up and where it should be slowed down and taken carefully – and all the other details.

When he is convinced that he understands the play the producer should start plotting the movements of each character as he or she enters or leaves the stage. Movement should not be included just for movement's sake. If a character is asked to move from one position to another the producer should have a reason for it. The various movements can be sketched in on the producer's script opposite the relevant dialogue.

A considerable amount of work can be done even before the play has been cast. The producer must make sure that he is familiar with his script and that he knows the exact size of the stage upon which the play is to be performed so he can plot the movements accurately. Then he can call auditions and cast the play.

As soon as the play is cast, if not before, the producer should assemble his backstage staff. He will need:

A scenic designer and scenery building crew This is where the arts and crafts departments of a senior school can be called into play. The designer should be given a copy of the play to read, make himself familiar with the possibilities of the stage and hall in which it is to be performed and then discuss the set with the producer. Unless there are excellent facilities and many keen and experienced workers the producer should keep the number of sets down to a minimum. Any change of scenery involves a great deal of work and can take a great deal of time. One really good set is worth six bad ones. If there are a number of scene changes in the play then one general purpose set could be designed. For the average school play the scenery will consist of a number of *flats*. A flat consists of canvas stretched across a framework of wood about a metre across. These extend across the back of the set and the required scene such as a wall of a house is painted across the set on all the flats. Any scenic designer who wants to learn how to design flats should read the relevant chapters in *Drama for Youth* by Richard Courtney (Pitman 1964).

A stage manager The task of the stage manager is to control everything that happens behind the scenes. He must see that all the props are in the right place, make sure that scenery and costumes are correct and that effects, lighting etc are in working order. He must also coordinate the work of all the other backstage workers.

The prompter The stage manager also sometimes assumes the prompter's role but this is not a good idea as he has far too much to do on the nights of the performances. Besides prompting is a full time job. The prompter should attend all the rehearsals if possible and make sure that his script contains all the cuts and effects introduced by the producer. During the performance he should be stationed in the wings where he can see and hear all the cast and not be distracted by the chaos around him. Sitting on top of a step ladder is a favourite position.

The call boy It is the duty of the call boy to see that the members of the cast are in the wings ready to make their entrances on time. He should have a marked copy of the script and be familiar with all the marked exits and entrances.

Make up artists There should be at least two make up artists for every production. It is their job to see that the basic stage make up is bought and available in sufficient quantities and to help the actors apply their make up. Basic make up should be applied in this fashion:

1 Wash the skin. Cover all areas to be made up with removing cream, remembering to grease behind the ears, all the visible neck and throat and up into the hair line.

2 Dry the skin with cotton wool and take off as much grease as possible.

3 Apply astringent lotion over the removing cream. The face should then be ready for grease paint.

4 Apply grease paint. This may be purchased in all colours and will vary according to the effect desired. For ordinary stage make up men should have a base of numbers 5 and 9 (yellow and brownish red). To emphasize cheek colouring number 9 should be used over the number 5. For women a base of number 2 (pink) for fair

complexions and 2½ (rose pink) for dark complexions is suitable. With experience the suitable shades for different skins will be found.
5 Powder over grease paint on face and apply liquid make up to hands.
6 After the production remove the make up with removing cream on cotton wool. Then wash with warm water and soap.

Lighting technician Stage lighting is a complex affair and should be kept extremely simple unless a member of staff is well versed in its technicalities. The lighting capabilities of the hall to be used should be explored before any plans are made to light the stage. Teachers wishing to learn more about lighting for the theatre should read *Stage Lighting* by F. Bentham (Pitman 1957) and *Stage Lighting for the Amateur Producer* by Angus Wilson (Pitman 1960).

Wardrobe mistress The wardrobe mistress is responsible for costuming the play. Clothes can often be specially hired for a costume play but it does help if the wardrobe mistress is capable of making or adapting clothes for the cast.

Producing the play

From the very start the producer should try to give the cast confidence by appearing to have everything in hand. He must always look as if he knows exactly what he is doing and he can help to give this impression by plotting out all the moves of the cast in advance, knowing where the scenery will be so that chairs can be used to simulate tables, doors and other parts of the set, and drawing up and adhering to a set routine for rehearsals.

At the first rehearsal the producer should give the cast his idea of what the play is about and the general effect he hopes to create. The cast should then read the play right through and discuss it afterwards. Not only will this give them some insight into the play but it will help to break down any barriers of shyness.

For the first few weeks the cast will rehearse with scripts in their hands, but even at this stage they should be making their correct entrances and moves on the stage which they write down as they are given by the producer. If the hall in which the production is to take place is not available for rehearsals these should take place on a simulated stage the same size as the real one and with the furniture, doors, windows, etc either chalked in or marked in some other way.

It will not be possible to go through the whole play during one normal rehearsal period so the producer should draw up a comprehensive rehearsal schedule and do his best to adhere to it. Those actors not in the section being rehearsed should be informed well in advance and not called upon to attend. Needless to say, all actors should be

TEACHERS WORLD
Junior school children on an out of school visit to a dairy in Bicester

Collecting specimens for analysis in the botany class

Junior school children try to identify leaves collected on a nature ramble

Worms may not be the most appealing of pets but they are easy to keep and can be used for a wide variety of topic work

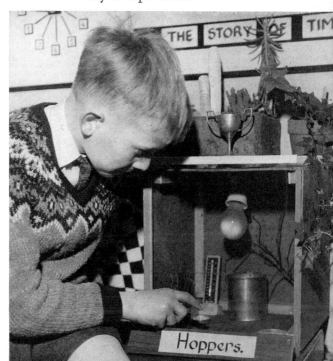

home made cage
ouses the grasshoppers

A secondary student tends the plants in the school greenhouse

encouraged to learn their lines as quickly as possible. Towards the end of the rehearsal period – say in the last two weeks before the production – rehearsals should be held more often and the whole play should be run through at a time. The day before the first public performance of the play there should be a dress rehearsal – a complete rehearsal involving costumes, make up, scenery, lighting etc.

Speaking

Some children who make their first contact with speaking before an audience at a drama club or in a school play become sufficiently interested in public speaking to join debating societies. Such societies can be extremely enjoyable and will help the children involved to gain confidence and learn how to speak on their feet.

Not all children will be able or willing to plunge into debates straight away and in the early days of a debating society the teacher in charge would be well advised to bring its members along gently. Meetings at which every member has to give a five minute talk of his or her own choice will provide good practice, so will mock trials. When full scale debates are launched care should be taken to see that they are properly organized. There should be a chairman, a motion to be debated, a proposer and seconder both for and against the motion, and arrangements for members to speak from the floor before the vote is taken.

Puppets and marionettes

One type of drama which is becoming increasingly popular in many schools is the puppet or marionette theatre. Marionettes are those puppets controlled by strings, the term 'puppet' is more general and embraces glove puppets etc.

It is perfectly possible for children to make their own puppets and marionettes and to construct the stages on which their creations may perform. In order to make a puppet the children will need plasticine or other modelling clay, newspaper, paste and brushes.

The modelling clay should be shaped into an oval, something like half an egg. A face should be modelled on the curved side, with deep holes for eyes and exaggerated nose, lips and chin. The newspapers should then be torn into very small pieces of paper. The modelling clay should be covered with paste and the curved side entirely covered with pieces of paper, slightly overlapping each other. Seven layers of paper should be used and then left to dry on the modelling clay.

A day or two later the clay can be disengaged from the paper and discarded. Each child then have a mask of a face made of paper. A rolled piece of cardboard will suffice for the neck. A piece of newspaper should be crumpled, pasted and put inside the face mask and the cardboard neck rested against it. More crumpled paper should be pasted around the neck and the whole strapped into place by strips of newspaper pasted round the completed head and neck. Again about seven layers will be needed at the back of the head which should then be left to dry. When dry the head may be painted. The children should be allowed a free choice in this direction. The way in which they decide to ornament the head will probably be influenced by the shape of the final version. At this point ears made of cardboard or similar material can be glued to the sides of the head and, if required, hair attached to the top.

When the head has been completed, a glove body should be attached to it. This body is made out of a piece of material which is attached to the head. A piece of circular cardboard should be fitted round the neck and the top of the material, which has a thread running round it with the two ends projecting, is placed round the neck and the ends of the thread are drawn tight, thus securing the body to the head.

In order to manipulate the head and body the hand is put into the glove with the index finger in the neck and the thumb and second finger in the two arms of the body and by manipulating the fingers and the thumb the head and body will move to order.

To build a puppet theatre a screen large enough to conceal the people working the puppets should be constructed. This need consist only of a piece of wood about 1 m high and 1½ m wide. On top of this screen a ledge should be constructed to act as the stage. Above and around this stage there should be a picture frame to depict the theatre, perhaps covered with curtain material. In order to present a play the children controlling the puppets crouch behind the screen and move the puppets above their heads on the stage.

A puppet theatre

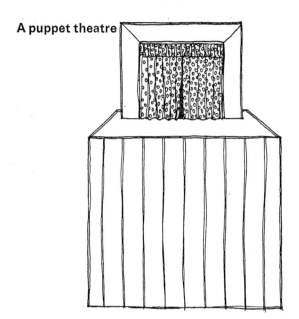

The children can be divided into groups to make up their own short puppet plays which they then perform on the stage.

References
1 R. N. Pemberton–Billing and J. D. Clegg *Teaching Drama* ULP 1965
2 Richard Courtney *Teaching Drama* Cassell 1965
3 *Drama in the Schools of Wales* HMSO 1954
4 D. E. Adland *Group Drama* Longmans 1964
5 Anne Driver *Music and Movement* OUP 1936

Further reading
E. J. Burton *Drama in Schools* Jenkins 1955
Peter Slade *Child Drama* ULP 1954
Richard Courtney *Drama for Youth* Pitman 1964
J. Wiles and A. Garrard *Leap to Life* Chatto and Windus 1957
Grace Brown *Mime in Schools and Clubs* Macdonald and Evans 1953
Rose Bruford *Speech and Drama* Methuen 1948
John Allen *Play Production* Dobson 1950
Yoti Lane *Stage Make Up* Hutchinson 1950

Elizabeth Morgan *A Practical Guide to Drama in the Primary School* Ward Lock Educational 1969
J. W. Casciani *Speak for Yourselves* Harrap 1967
Peter Chilvers *Talking, Discussion, Improvisation and Debate in Schools* Batsford 1968
Keith Dadds *On Speaking Terms* E. J. Arnold 1966

4

Careers

Advising boys and girls who are about to leave school on the possible careers and areas of further training and education open to them is a highly specialized affair which properly should be left to a trained careers master or youth counsellor, preferably one with wide and varied experience of industry and the professions and who is in constant touch with the changing circumstances and requirements in the world of business. Unfortunately this vital and intricate task all too often is delegated to a member of the staff as an extra curricular activity, or at best as something to be tackled in a number of free periods allocated for the purpose.

It cannot be too strongly emphasized that the post of careers master should be a full time one and that the holder of the post should be specially trained at one of the youth counselling courses run at such universities as Keele, Reading, Exeter etc. Such a teacher, with no classroom responsibilities, should have time to keep in touch with the requirements of universities and colleges, the changing demands and qualifications needed for the various trades and professions, and so on.

If however as is highly likely, the post of careers master or mistress in a school is largely an honorary one performed as an out of school activity, there are a number of courses which may be followed in order to fit the teacher for the post at least temporarily.

Liaison with students
The careers teacher must know the boys and girls being advised. This is a self evident fact but one that should be stated at the outset. If the careers teacher meets a good number of the pupils of the school during ordinary school activities then he or she will already have some knowledge of the child's abilities, personality and perhaps even ambitions. This knowledge must be implemented by discussions with the teachers who teach the child regularly, examination of the child's school reports and other data and, most important, by interviewing the child not once but on a number of occasions during the child's last year at school.

For this purpose the careers teacher should have an office in which to conduct the interviews and keep files and other records. It would be asking too much to expect secretarial assistance even in the most enlightened school – in many cases even the headteacher has to make do with part time help in this direction – but there should be somewhere where the careers teacher can conduct interviews and hold discussions. If a permanent office is available then careers posters may be displayed on the walls and pamphlets and other literature kept available.

The careers teacher should be readily available should children want to discuss their problems. If the teacher in question is carrying a full work load as far as teaching duties are concerned then this will not be easy, but if the teacher can make a point of staying behind in the careers room or some other accessible but reasonably private place for an hour or so every evening it will be a great help.

The careers teacher should not, of course, rely upon the student seeking him or her out. As has been stated, all school leavers should be interviewed at regular intervals, their school records checked and each pupil discussed with other teachers and, if possible, with parents. Long before the end of the final school year the teacher should have a good idea of what the child wants, whether he or she is capable of fulfilling that ambition and whether it is possible to help the child. A report should be written on each child and this can be used when it comes to filling in the forms submitted by the Careers Service which will be discussed later in this chapter.

Obtaining professional help

Every careers teacher whether part time or full time should accept as much professional advice as possible when it comes to helping school leavers find suitable employment. In most areas the most useful contacts in this field are the local Careers Advisory Service and the youth employment officer. The address of the local Careers Advisory Service may be obtained from the Education Department or the town hall and the careers master or mistress should try to meet the youth employment officer as quickly as possible and find out the range of services he can offer.

The youth employment officer and the various careers advisory officers are professionals. They know, or can find out, just what careers opportunities there are locally or nationally, what qualifications are needed, what the prospects are and so on. The sooner the careers teacher calls the Careers Advisory Service into the school the better it is for all concerned. Some careers teachers start bringing in members of the Advisory Service during the penultimate year of the child's school life, so that by the time the child takes GCE or CSE both the Careers Advisory Service and the school staff know both the capabilities and ambitions of the individual children. The fact that their jobs after school are being discussed and thought about often acts as a spur to many children, especially those less academically gifted, who now see a concrete reason for working hard.

Another source of outside help which may be called upon if needed is the Child Guidance Centre which can provide specialist help in the field of psychology and psychiatry should it be needed.

Collaboration with employers

Although the Careers Advisory Service and the local youth employment officer will both provide the careers teacher with a great deal of practical assistance it must be remembered that these officials will be helping in a great number of schools in one particular area and that they cannot devote all their time to one school. This means that it is still incumbent upon the careers teacher to familiarize himself with the latest developments in the careers field.

There are a number of ways in which this may be done. Most large industries and business concerns supply pamphlets and leaflets about career opportunities in the organizations concerned. The addresses to write to can be found in any careers supplement in the educational or national press. The careers teacher can then file one copy of each pamphlet and display or distribute others to interested children.

Other sources of literature describing career opportunities may be obtained from trade associations, careers conferences, trade unions and from the Careers Advisory Service.

If it is at all possible the careers teacher should arrange visits for parties of school leavers to local factories and other organizations. The careers teacher should accompany the children on these visits as often as possible for, as the Newsom Report says: 'a major problem is how to ensure that the teachers themselves, apart from having the right contacts and the necessary sources of information, really understand the work situation as their pupils will meet it.' A few short visits will not necessarily provide the teacher with that knowledge but such excursions will have their value.

Another source of contact with different trades and professions is provided by inviting representatives to visit the school and give talks. Some organizations provide professional public relations officers to undertake this task and these often provide highly professional talks, sometimes illustrated with slides and even films, but the careers teacher should try and provide a balanced picture and talks from ordinary rank and file members of a firm can often prove just as illuminating as a prepared sales talk, sometimes more so!

It goes without saying that the careers teacher should be particularly knowledgeable about the prevailing local employment conditions and such information can usually be acquired by talking to the youth employment officer.

Books and television

There are a great many books on the market designed to help both the careers teacher and children eager to learn more about different careers. Some are more helpful than others.

The publications of the Careers Research and Advisory Centre are always sensible and comprehensive. Particularly useful are *Middle School Choice* (1967), a guide to GCE and CSE requirements for various professions and *Yearbook of Education and Training Opportunities* (1969/70), an extremely comprehensive guide. Another publication of the Careers Research and Advisory Centre of particular value to careers teachers is its *Handbook of Recruitment Literature* (1968), which will help any teacher in his or her efforts to compile and evaluate the leaflets and pamphlets issued by trades, professions and industries.

The Central Youth Employment Executive also offers some extremely helpful booklets especially the *Choice of Careers* series which covers a wide range of individual careers with a separate pamphlet for each job. The same organization also publishes a more general *Careers Guide* (HMSO 1968), which is recommended.

Other official or semi official guides are *A Compendium of Advanced Courses in Technical Colleges* (1968) issued by the Regional Advisory Councils in England and Wales which describes the requirements for entry to technical colleges, *Signposts to Higher Education* (HMSO) and *University and College Entrance: the Basic Facts* (NUT 1968).

Two good if expensive guide books which ought to be in the school library if not the careers office are *Yearbook of Technical Education and Careers in Industry* by H. C. Dent (Black, reprinted 1967) and *British Qualifications*, by Barbara Priestley (Deutsch 1966).

A number of publishers issue career books for school leavers. The best in my experience are those issued by Educational Explorers under the general heading of *My Life and Work*. These books are distinguished by the fact that they are written by members of the profession being examined and are marked by a realism and enthusiasm lacking in even the best of most other careers series. Other publishers who provide sound and accurate careers series, are Evans, Robert Hale, Cornmarket Press, Gollancz, Lutterworth and Bodley Head.

Careers teachers should also make use of the schools television series on careers provided both by ITV and the BBC.

Two different activities pursued at outward bound schools. Above rock climbing and below camping on the high fells

St John Ambulance cadets giving first aid to a volunteer victim

ST JOHN AMBULANCE BRIGADE

5

Journeys and excursions

Any association with out of school activities requires that the teacher concerned should like and get on with children, but when it comes to taking part in journeys and excursions this attribute becomes even more important. If the teacher is going to spend hours, days or even weeks with children, then he or she must first determine whether this is going to be a pleasant experience or a deadly chore. Should it seem like the latter then the teacher should give up all thoughts of organizing an expedition. Any teacher embarking on a school journey or expedition should have a good relationship with the children coming on the trip. Even over a relatively short period of time with everything going swimmingly, the unnaturally close proximity of teacher and taught can be a strain; over a longer period or when things begin to come adrift, unless both parties get on well it can be a disaster!

Journeys abroad
Once only senior schools went on school journeys abroad but now primary schools are going in ever increasing numbers and there is nothing to stop such a journey being a rewarding and enjoyable experience for younger boys and girls as well as older ones if it is well planned and properly organized.

The first thing of course is to select the area to be visited. A number of factors can influence this choice. The children can be studying a particular country or the teacher may have received good reports of a journey made there by another school, or there may be a particular goal in mind – a visit to the Louvre or the tulip fields of Holland and so on.

Once the teacher has decided upon the destination the headteacher of the school should be consulted and if there is no objection from this quarter the children in the school can be canvassed to see if there if enough initial enthusiasm to make the project a viable proposition. Should the children seem eager the next step is to call a meeting of parents and staff to discuss ways and means.

At this meeting the assembled adults should be informed of the destination, the reasons for the trip and the advantages it offers to the children. No concrete propositions should be made at this preliminary gathering but if the parents present seem interested the teacher responsible for the organization may then promise to collect details of cost, route, etc and to report back to the parents at a later date.

Now the teacher may go ahead and assemble as much data as possible. It is at this stage that the problem of whether or not to use the services of a travel agent should be decided. There are a number of advantages in employing a professional agent who will cope with all the details. A good agent will be experienced and have up to date knowledge of the area to be visited. If he specializes in school travel, as many do, he will know all the problems to be solved. Some of the larger firms can provide representatives to come along to the school and give talks, often illustrated with films and slides, about the country in question. Many firms have representatives in the countries to be visited who are available to smooth out any difficulties or last minute hitches. Another factor in favour of using a reputable agent is that he is often able to offer a much cheaper tour than would be possible for the teacher to arrange. The agent can obtain discounts for block bookings and pass on these savings to his customers. Most agents, incidentally, offer a free place on the tour to every teacher accompanied by a certain number of paying pupils – this number can vary from ten to twenty-five according to the agent.

It should be borne in mind that these advantages are only offered by efficient and reputable agencies. If a school is unlucky enough to fall into the hands of an inefficient or disreputable organization the trip can be misery from beginning to end. In order to avoid this the teacher should obtain the brochures of as many different agents as possible, study them carefully and compare them with each other. Other schools which have had successful journeys in the past should be canvassed about the ability of the agents they employed. Membership of the Association of British Travel Agents is a sign that the agency in question has reached a certain qualifying standard, although a number of good firms have not yet joined the Association.

If the teacher does decide to use the services of a travel agency and has made his choice of firm he can then consult the agency and obtain from them a rough estimate of the cost per head of the proposed trip, especially if he can give the agent a rough idea of the number of children and adults likely to be coming on the trip. The teacher should ask the agent to include in this costing the price of a comprehensive insurance policy, covering accidents, sickness, etc on the journey. Almost all agents will provide such a policy at a reasonable price.

Armed with this knowledge the teacher can call another meeting of parents and staff and tell them how long the journey will take, the route it will cover and the likely price. The parents should then be given time to think it over and asked to write to the teacher if they want their child or children to go on the trip.

Before the teacher starts preparing the children for the journey he or she should make quite sure that the names of the children coming on the expedition have been entered on a list. Every parent should write to the teacher guaranteeing to pay the agreed cost of the journey, either in a lump sum or by weekly or monthly payments. The parent should also agree in writing not to hold the teacher responsible for any mishaps on the journey.

A number of adult helpers, either other teachers or parents, should also be recruited for the journey. If the party is a mixed one there should be an adult of either sex and the more adults the better.

Once the children coming on the trip have been identified and have either paid their fares in advance or started bringing the money in regularly, the teacher should form a travel club for these children. In order to make the most of this the trip should be organized a good time in advance, perhaps even several terms. Not only will this enable the travel club to cover a variety of activities but it will also give the children from poorer homes more time to save the necessary money.

The travel club should be held regularly and be devoted to preparing the children for their forthcoming trip. They should learn as much as they can about the areas they are going to visit and with this end in mind they should prepare folders for the journey and muster as much information as they can – route, places of interest, currency, geography, history, natural history etc. Space should be left in the folders for information to be added while the children are actually on their journey.

People with personal knowledge of the area to be seen should be encouraged to visit the club and talk about their experiences. The children should be given practice in using the currency of the foreign country.

Whether the services of a travel agency are being employed or the teacher is arranging the tour himself passports should be obtained for all the prospective travellers. They may be applied for on forms obtainable from the Passport Offices in London, Liverpool or Glasgow or any Ministry of Labour office. Most travel agencies will handle this for the school but may charge extra for doing so. The forms should be filled in, the names of guarantors inserted and then returned with two copies of a recent photograph and the fee. Passports are issued for a period of five years initially and may be renewed. Enquiries should be made in case a visa as well as a passport is needed.

All means of travel have their supporters. To travel by train or coach can be tiring but is cheaper than going by air. Perhaps the most suitable form of transport for schools is by coach, especially if the route is so arranged that there is no night travel, because at least in a coach all the children are together under the supervision of the teachers in charge.

In order to obtain a list of travel agents, especially those specializing in school journeys, study the pages of the educational press. Firms which have been recommended by teachers as having given value for money in the past include:

Young Travellers, 212 Addington Road, Selsdon, South Croydon, Surrey

ETA Tours, Oakfield House, Haywards Heath, Sussex

European College Tours, 10 Hans Crescent, Knightsbridge, London SW1

BUS School Travel Association, 165 Kensington High Street, London W8

School Journey Association of London, 23 Southampton Place, London WC1

School Travel Service, 4 Culloden Road, Enfield, Middlesex

For more specialized services the British India Steam Navigation Company, 1 Aldgate, London EC3, among others provides educational cruises for children.

A comprehensive first aid kit should be taken with the party and a ratio of at least one adult to every ten children is essential. It should be remembered that reciprocal national health service arrangements are in force only with Bulgaria, Denmark, Norway, Sweden and Yugoslavia and that medical attention can be costly in other countries, so a sickness insurance policy should be taken out for the party. Addresses and telephone numbers along the route should be given to parents, and the addresses and telephone numbers of parents obtained so that there can be swift and easy contact between both parties if necessary.

Travel in Great Britain
When it comes to arranging school journeys in Great Britain the following addresses may be of use to the teacher:

Automobile Association, Home Routes Department, Fanum House, High Street, Teddington, Middlesex

Royal Automobile Club, 83 Pall Mall, London SW1

Cyclists' Touring Club, 13 Spring Street, London W2

Association of Agriculture, 78 Buckingham Gate, London SW1

Central Office of Information, Hercules Road, Westminster Bridge Road, London SE1

London Transport Publicity Office, Griffith House, 280 Old Marylebone Road. London NW1

Port of London Authority, Public Relations Officer, Trinity Square, PO Box 242, London EC3

Youth Hostels Association, Trevelyan House, St Albans, Hertfordshire

   If asked these organizations will provide a list of the services they offer to aid travelling and touring parties in Great Britain.

Before embarking on any school journey at home or abroad, the teacher should be quite clear about his responsibilities. Although the journey may well take place out of school hours his duty to the children in his care is just as pronounced as it would be in the school or playground. At all times the teacher is *in loco parentis*. H. C. Barnard sums up this situation in *An Introduction to Teaching* when he writes:

> Your immediate considerations should be: What action would a sensible parent take? . . . . Suppose, however, that you are away from school, in charge of a team which is playing an away match, or on a school journey or expedition, and some accident to a pupil occurs. You are still on duty and responsible for those in your charge. It is therefore always wise, whenever there is the slightest doubt, to call in medical aid without delay. It is safer to err on the side of fussiness; for if you fail to send for the doctor and unpleasant results ensue, you may be held to have been negligent.[1]

School journeys in Great Britain can take a number of forms, ranging from a nature walk to a fortnight's summer camp. Whatever the function the same basic rules should be followed by the teacher as hold good for expeditions abroad. Travelling should be organized well in advance. Trains provide the fastest form of transport once air travel is ruled out but coaches have the advantage of being more independent and keeping all the children together under the eye of the teachers in charge.

   It should be remembered that some children suffer from travel sickness and precautions should be taken to guard against this. There are a number of travel sickness pills which may be obtained from chemists without prescription. The teacher is not recommended to emulate the senior mistress of my first school who, when much against her will was persuaded to accompany a coach load of children on a day trip round the Isle of Wight, boarded the coach carrying a large bucket, surveyed the children with a gimlet eye and indicating the bucket said: 'You all know what this is for, and I'll slap the legs of the first child who has to use it.'

These days school journeys are regarded as an essential part of the education of any boy or girl and most teachers do their best to include exploration in any project or topic work they may attempt. Some of the more common destinations are mentioned below.

Museums and art galleries
Teachers will be familiar with the museums and art galleries in their own neighbourhood. For details of museums all over Great Britain they are recommended to read: *Museums and Galleries in Great Britain* Index Publications (published annually).

There are of course many first rate provincial galleries and museums but for sheer scope and variety those of London would be difficult to beat, not only for general purposes but also for specialist material. Among many museums and galleries worth a visit in the capital are:
British Museum Great Russell Street, London WC1 Open Monday–Saturday: 10 a.m.–5 p.m. Sunday: 2.30–6 p.m. Tours accompanied by lecturers are available. Enquiries should be made to the Director.
British Museum (Natural History) Cromwell Road, London SW7 Public lecture tours are held daily at 3 p.m.
Commonwealth Institute Kensington High Street, London W8 School parties catered for, film shows etc.
Geological Survey and Museum Exhibition Road, London SW7 Demonstrations and tours arranged for school parties.
London Museum Kensington Palace, London W8 Lecture tours arranged for school parties.
National Gallery Trafalgar Square, London WC2
National Maritime Museum Greenwich, London SE10 Lecture tours arranged for school parties.
National Postal Museum King Edward Building, GPO, London EC1 Lecture tours arranged for school parties.
Science Museum Exhibition Road, South Kensington, London SW7 Lectures and demonstrations arranged for school parties.
Tate Gallery Millbank, London SW1 Lectures arranged for school parties.
Victoria and Albert Museum Cromwell Road, South Kensington, London SW7 Lectures arranged for school parties.

Outside London museums and galleries of particular interest include:
Bath *American Museum in Britain* Claverton Manor BA2 7BD Comprehensive exhibition of Americana.
Christchurch *Red House Museum and Art Gallery* Quay Road, BH23 1BU Natural History, antiquities and nineteenth century costume.
Haslemere *Educational Museum* High Street Natural history and geology.
Huddersfield *Tolson Memorial Museum* Ravensknowle Park, Huddersfield HD5 8D Local history and natural science.

Leeds *City Museum* Municipal Buildings Leeds LS1 3AA
Leicester *Museum and Art Gallery* New Walk, LEI 6TD
Liverpool *City of Liverpool Museums* William Brown Street,
Liverpool L3 8EN.
Luton *Museum and Art Gallery* Wardown Park Regional collection.
Manchester *Manchester Museum* The University, Oxford Road,
Manchester M13 9WJ
Middlesbrough *Dorman Museum and Municipal Art Gallery*
Newcastle Upon Tyne *Natural History Society, Hancock Museum*
Barras Bridge, Newcastle Upon Tyne NE2 4PT
Nottinghamshire *Schools Museum* Gedling House, Newark
Scunthorpe *Borough Museum and Art Gallery* Oswald Road
Sheffield *City Museum* Weston Park, Sheffield S10 2TP
Somerset *County Museum* Taunton
Warwick *County Museum* Market Place Geology, natural history.
Aberdeen *Art Gallery and Museum* Schoolhill AB9 1FQ
Edinburgh *Schools Museum Service* City of Edinburgh Education
Department, St Giles Street, Edinburgh EH1 1YW
Glasgow *Museum and Art Gallery* Kelvingrove, Glasgow C3
Cardiff *National Museum of Wales* Cathays Park CF1 3NP

Teachers wishing to arrange a conducted tour of one of the above
museums should write well in advance of the proposed visit to see if a
guide will be available. In touring museums as with most other places
of interest, a great deal of time will be saved if the children are briefed
well in advance and told what to look out for when they arrive. In
addition to providing background material for their class work a
successful trip to a museum might well encourage the children to start
their own local history or geological museum at the school.

Exploring the neighbourhood

One of the most interesting and useful ways of incorporating excursions
and visits into the timetable is by using them to gather material for a
project on the children's own neighbourhood. This project may be
extended or limited at will – from an examination of the streets
surrounding the school to a comprehensive study of the town or village.
Visits to gather material for such a project could be arranged to:
Local factories and businesses The larger organizations like the post office,
the fire station and similar organizations will be better equipped to deal
with school visits, but most firms will cooperate if given plenty of
warning and approached in the right way. With older children such
expeditions can also serve to help them to make up their minds about
their careers.

Theatres and places of entertainment Cinemas, sports stadia and other places of entertainment always appeal to children and help spark off their enthusiasm for project work.

Local transport organizations Bus depots, railway stations and docks and airports may all be included under this heading. The children should obtain copies of timetables etc.

Churches and buildings of historic interest If there are any stately homes in the area open to the public they should be included in the visits.

Local flora and fauna Nature walks are always of interest to children. Organizing a nature ramble will be discussed in a later chapter.

Local amenities The public health service, water supply, gas and electricity should all be investigated in any project on the neighbourhood.

Any school journey can be made an interesting and enjoyable experience as long as a few simple rules are obeyed. Trips should be organized well in advance and nothing left to chance. Letters asking permission to make the trip should be written to the necessary authorities several months in advance and confirmed a week or two before the trip. Transport should be arranged and booked. The children should be prepared for the trip by being given full details of the route, timing, etc. They should also be briefed in the etiquette of a school journey; they will be representing the school and should set an example of behaviour and dress. Any necessary equipment – note books, sample boxes and so on, should be prepared and taken on the trip. The children should be given plenty of opportunities to ask questions and ample time in which to make their preparations. It goes without saying that any help from outside organizations or individuals should be acknowledged immediately by teacher and pupils in the form of a letter of thanks.

There are many possible destinations for a school journey and the preparations and follow up activities will differ for each one but a few sample expeditions are outlined below.

A port or harbour

There are some three hundred ports in Great Britain, about ninety of which are licensed to handle imports from overseas. About three hundred million tons of goods pass through British ports in a year. Any class engaged in a project on ships and shipping, trade, imports and exports, transport etc would benefit from a trip to a port or harbour.

Arranging permission to make the trip The harbour master, ports authority or dockyard superintendent of the port in question should be approached in writing asking for permission to visit the harbour on a certain day. The teacher should give the date, expected time of arrival, time of departure, number in party and ages of children. If permission is forthcoming the teacher can then see about making arrangements.

Organizing transport Arrangements should be made with a private coach firm or the railway booking office if the port is some distance away.

Searching for helpers If there are more than eight children in the party the teacher should find at least one other adult to accompany him on the expedition.

Preparing the children The children should be given a brief outline of the background of the port they are going to see and an itinerary of the trip. The major ports of Great Britain are London, Liverpool, Hull, Clydeport, Southampton and Bristol but many smaller ports are of equal importance, Portsmouth would be a suitable port to visit.

The children should also be given some background information on ports in general. Many changes are taking place in British ports today, oil pipe lines may harm coastal tanker trade, road and rail freight are both taking away business from ports. In order to survive ports are having to streamline their methods and increase their efficiency. Once many smaller ports were kept going by the demand for coal which was mainly shipped from port to port. Today the demand for coal has diminished with a subsequent falling off in traffic. Lately there has been a significant increase in bulk cargo trades. This means that cargo ships are growing larger and can only use ports with deep water harbours.

On the other hand, there is an increase in trade with western Europe, so east coast ports of Great Britain, even the smaller ones, are on the whole doing better than the ports on the west coast. To facilitate rapid loading and unloading a great deal of fresh equipment has been installed in many ports.

The children should be told to bear these points in mind and when they reach the port they should try and find out whether the port seems busy or slack. Does the equipment seem new or old fashioned? Are there facilities for specialized cargo like oil or coal? What European and other ports does this particular harbour serve? Is it a deep water harbour?

The children should also be encouraged to try and find out who owns the port they are going to visit. Some ports are nationalized transport undertakings administered by the British Transport Docks Board, others are run by statutory trusts or local authorities, while a few are owned by private companies.

Whatever the ownership, the revenue of a port comes from the charges and dues paid by vessels using the harbour and its facilities. A ship pays a charge according to its size or tonnage. It also pays, in many cases, for such facilities as channel lighting, being towed and the services of a pilot. The children should try and find out as much as possible about the help a ship gets from the port when it docks there.

They should also try and make a study of all the people working in the port – dock labourers and officials, customs officers, lighthouse workers, Trinity House officials, harbour police, port authorities etc.

Some children could be detailed to find out how the port is administered and maintained. The following jobs could be investigated: dredging, surveying and charting the tideway, maintenance of approach channels, removal of wrecks and obstructions, prevention of pollution, regulation of traffic, supervision of the foreshore, provision and maintenance of moorings and so on.

Other children could concentrate on finding out as much as possible about the equipment of the average port. The main piece of equipment in general use is the quay crane or the ship's crane, although it is the shore crane which is more commonly used. The weight these cranes are capable of supporting range from about a tonne to over two hundred tonnes. In some ports these are diesel electric cranes running on rails while others have special coal loading and unloading piers. There are also special timber quays and larger ports have suction machines for moving grain cargoes. Facilities for moving oil are provided by the oil companies.

The children should be given a brief outline of the sort indicated above, if possible illustrated with pictures or lantern slides. They should be allowed to decide for themselves which particular aspect of dock life they are going to concentrate on when they make the trip, and then find out in advance as much as they can about their chosen topic. Note books should be prepared in advance as well as a list of questions to ask.

Making the trip How the trip itself is conducted will depend upon the facilities provided by the port in question. If a guide has been delegated to take the children round they can ask him questions and ask to be shown the areas they are particularly interested in. If there is no guide the teacher and his adult helpers will have to do their best to cope with the demands of the children.

Follow up activities When the children return to school they should be given every chance to consolidate their knowledge, to prepare notebooks, displays, pictures etc. For more detailed help in preparing project activities teachers are recommended to read:
Peter Rance *Teaching by Topics* Ward Lock Educational 1968
Graeme Kent *Projects in the Primary School* Batsford 1968

A fire station
A visit to a fire station is usually popular with boys and girls and may

be incorporated into a project on the fire brigade in particular or on the various social services in general.

Preparation The usual preparation should be undertaken, including obtaining the permission of the local chief officer, arranging transport facilities etc.

Encouraging the children Before the trip is made the children should be given the general background of the fire service in Great Britain. It will help in all preparatory project work if the children are given advance information under various headings. They can then choose which particular headings they want to concentrate on when the project gets under way. As far as the fire service is concerned, the following divisions will usually be found satisfactory:

History

Roman Times Organized Roman fire fighting service probably operated in Britain. This organization was equipped to deal with fires and was known as the corps of *Vigiles*.

Roman Times–1668 After the Romans left Britain there were no organized fire fighting services for almost fifteen hundred years. Fires were attacked by private citizens with leather buckets, ladders and handsquirts provided by property owners or municipal authorities. The Great Fire of London (1666) showed that efficient professional fire fighting services were necessary.

1668 First fire insurance office founded. By 1680 several of these offices had established their own fire brigades. At first a brigade would only attempt to put out a fire at establishments insured by the office to which it belonged. Later, however, a number of amalgamations took place.

1824 A municipal fire brigade was established in Edinburgh, followed in 1828 by one in Manchester. In most places, however, volunteer services continued to be the order of the day.

1832 The combined insurance company brigades were formed into the London Fire Engine Establishment. An official from each insurance company contributing to this establishment was put onto the supervisory committee.

1866 The London Fire Engine Establishment was taken over by the London public authority – the Metropolitan Board of Works. This was the first fire brigade in the country to be under the command of a municipal authority.

1866–1937 Local volunteer fire fighting institutions continued to be formed for some years after 1866, but gradually throughout the country the local authorities took over the responsibility for maintaining a service to prevent and fight fires.

1937–38 Volunteers were called for to join the Auxiliary Fire Service. These men trained in their spare time to fight fires in case of a war.

1938 The Fire Brigades Act created fire authorities throughout Great Britain, requiring them to provide fire fighting organizations for the areas under their control.

1939–45 In the second world war the fire brigades and the Auxiliary Fire Service did magnificent work in fighting fires after air raids, particularly during the blitz. In 1941 the fire brigades and the Auxiliary Fire Service were amalgamated into a single organization.

Present organization Today all areas of Great Britain are covered by fire fighting services. Each local authority is responsible for maintaining a service and there are about 135 local fire brigades in England and Wales. Each brigade is under the supervision of the local fire authority and it is the duty of the authority to:

1 maintain a fire brigade of sufficient strength to meet efficiently all normal requirements
2 secure the efficient training of members of the brigade
3 provide efficient means for dealing with fire calls and for summoning members of the brigade
4 make regulations prescribing qualifications for appointment and promotion
5 obtain information required for fire fighting purposes in respect of property in their area (this includes information on the character of the buildings, the available water supplies, means of access and allied matters)
6 organize salvage operations for the mitigation of damage which might result from fire fighting operations
7 provide arrangements for giving advice, on request, on fire prevention and means of escape in case of fire
8 join in schemes of mutual assistance with other authorities for supplementing the normal fire fighting service in special circumstances or in the event of large fires
9 take all reasonable measures for ensuring the provision of an adequate supply of water in case of fire

Vehicles and equipment The amount of equipment needed for fire fighting is varied. The main items present in every fire station are:

1 Pump escapes and pump ladders – these are driven by petrol or diesel engines. A water tank containing at least 454 litres of water and providing an immediate supply to one or more hose reels is built into the bodywork of the pump. The wheeled escape is carried on the appliance and consists of ladders in three sections extended by steel cables.

2 Turntable ladders – these ladders are mounted on turntables and can be rotated through part or the whole of a circle. The ladder can be extended to a height of 33 metres.
3 Water tenders – these consist of large water tanks capable of holding over 1000 litres and a small pump.
4 Emergency tenders – these are designed to carry such essential items of equipment as generators for providing lights at fires, resuscitation equipment and breathing equipment.
5 Hose laying lorries – these lorries are equipped with long lines of hose in case there is no handy source of water.

Training firemen A man joining the fire service will receive comprehensive fire fighting training at a centre provided by his local authority or a neighbouring authority. He will learn, in addition to basic fire fighting techniques, first aid, basic principles of building construction, hydraulics, electricity, physics, chemistry, fire brigade law and history and, often, motor driving, use of special appliances and equipment and other relevant activities.

Experienced fire officers can go to the Fire Service College at Dorking and its annexe at Moreton-in-Marsh for advanced training. Here they will study such subjects as chemistry, building construction, water supplies, electricity, fire appliances etc.

Service in a fire brigade To be a good fireman a recruit has to be fit and intelligent and possess a cool head. As a rule he should be between the ages of 18 and 30. The ranks in the fire service of England and Wales are (starting from the bottom) fireman, leading fireman, subofficer, station officer, assistant divisional officer, divisional officer grade III, divisional officer grade II, divisional officer grade I, assistant chief officer, chief officer. Firemen have to pass written examinations in various subjects as well as practical tests before they can be promoted in the lower ranks.

Firemen work in shifts which vary from one area to another and are assisted in some areas by part time firemen.

Fighting a fire Most appeals for help to the fire service are made by telephone. Most areas have an emergency number, such as 999, which may be dialled when the fire service is needed. Some districts also have public fire alarm systems.

The call is received in the fire station watchroom and is reported to the appropriate headquarters. A chart is maintained in the station watchroom and the headquarters control room on which the number of appliances sent to the fire is noted. If the fire should prove beyond the resources of a division, help will be sent from another division or, if it is closer, from another authority. Most fire brigades operate two-way radio systems to enable them to report progress and seek help.

Carrying out the project If the children are supplied with the above information under the appropriate headings well in advance it will help them to decide which areas they want to concentrate on. During their visit to the station they can ask questions and afterwards make their charts, notes, models etc.

A farm

A visit to a farm is usually appreciated, especially by urban children. Some schools in urban areas make and maintain contact with a rural school and arrange for the children to visit each other. In this way a town child gets a chance to see the countryside while a rural child may visit a town or city.

A visit to a farm may be tied up with projects on agriculture, animals, foodstuffs, milk etc. The usual arrangements should be made in advance of the visit and the children given the following background information and told to look out for the things mentioned when they make their visit to the farm.

Farms in Great Britain There are about 450,000 agricultural holdings in the United Kingdom but many of these are small, part time holdings. It is estimated that there are in the region of 42,000 large commercial farm businesses, 66,000 small commercial farm businesses and another 112,000 farm businesses providing a living for their occupants.

Types of farming Most farms include a variety of crops and livestock but there are four main types of farming in Great Britain.

Dairy farming This includes milk, butter and cheese production. Of the three, liquid milk is the most lucrative. The average consumption of milk in Great Britain is 2·8 litres per head per week. The average cow produces 3705 litres of milk in a year. Freedom from tuberculosis, once a scourge of farmers, has reduced wastage considerably. The production of milk has been improved by the development of grazing techniques, new methods of making high quality hay etc. All milk produced for sale in the United Kingdom has to be sold to or through one of the five milk marketing boards and a price guarantee is implemented through these boards.

Crops The main crops grown on British farms are:

Wheat The advent of new strains of wheat has led to greatly increased production in England. The widespread use of combine harvesters has made it necessary to bring in drying and storage facilities on many farms.

Barley Barley is grown both to be malted and to be sold as animal food. In the last ten years the production of barley in the United Kingdom has doubled.

Oats This crop is in a state of partial decline at the moment. It is no longer needed for horses and cannot compete with barley as a food for animals.

Fodder roots This is another crop being grown less and less. Kale is still grown in some quantity but both turnips and mangolds are in decline.

Sugar beet This is a crop grown mainly in East Anglia and Lincolnshire. This is where most of the sugar beet factories are situated. The crop is sponsored by the British Sugar Corporation which guarantees to buy the beet at previously agreed prices.

Potatoes Improved production methods have seen to it that while the amount of land devoted to growing potatoes has decreased, the number of potatoes grown has increased. Early potatoes are grown in many parts of England and Wales and marketed in the summer months. The later major crop is grown mainly is Essex, Lincolnshire and Yorkshire and is stored before sale. Northern Ireland produces enough potatoes for its own consumption and for export.

Livestock farming This is a specialized type of farming and can be divided up in the following ways:

Beef cattle There has been some decrease in the consumption of beef in the United Kingdom compared with the pre-war level but many beef cattle are still kept. Many beef cattle are marketed at about 12 months of age and some at 18 months of age. A great deal of beef derives from dairy herds. Some hardy beef herds are grazed in highland regions.

Sheep Good pasture land and increasingly effective veterinary measures against disease makes the United Kingdom a good sheep rearing area. More than 30 different varieties are to be found and while the production of wool is important most sheep are kept for the ultimate production of fat lambs.

Pigs People in Great Britain consume twice as much pork per head as they did before the war. Pigs are kept today for curing as bacon, consumption as pork and manufacture into sausages.

Poultry This has become a highly specialized industry. Great Britain has several flocks of over 100,000 birds, and most of the birds on farms are in flocks in excess of 1,000. An important section of the industry is the breeding of special table chickens or broilers.

Horticultural crops This is a small but valuable section of British farming. Market gardens have sprung up around most large cities and in the rural areas of Bedfordshire, Cambridgeshire, Hampshire and Kent.

Government assistance The government is assisted in a number of ways by the Ministry of Agriculture, Fisheries and Food. Each February the Ministry decides what prices will be paid in the forthcoming year for animals and crops. Farmers are also encouraged to grow crops by being granted subsidies so that they do not lose money by so doing. In approved cases the government will guarantee bank loans made to farmers. The government also assists farmers in marketing their products.

History of farming

3000 BC First farming folk land on the shores of Britain. They bring with them from the continent of Europe dogs, sheep, cattle, goats and pigs. In clay pots are seeds of wheat and barley. Their few tools are of stone, wood and bone. Succeeding generations of invaders bring refinements to the farming processes.

600 AD Saxons give up their warlike ways and settle to farming. They build collections of huts by rivers and share large field outside village fence. On this land they keep cows for meat and milk and graze sheep and pigs. Most villages share a plough pulled by oxen.

1300 Much of English land given over to grazing sheep. English wool trade famous. Most countrymen are allowed to work their own patch of ground as long as they give regular service on the land of the local lord of the manor. Common ground is farmed on the open field principle. Four large open fields given over to common use. Each year one field rested, the other three used.

1725–1795 Robert Bakewell revolutionized English farming. Specializing in breeding of cattle, sheep and horses he became renowned for the proportion of meat to bone on his animals. His Longhorn cattle and New Leicester sheep become famous all over Europe. By 1800 English livestock renowned.

1800–present day Steady growth of British farming.

Before the children make their trip to the farm they should be given the information detailed above and allowed time to make up their minds as to which area they are going to concentrate on. Then the trip may be made and the customary follow up work undertaken.

The town hall

A visit to the town hall or local municipal buildings should be included in any project on local government. There are so many aspects of this subject that more than one trip may be necessary. Before the first of the trips the children should be given the following information divided up into subject headings:

Types of local government There are a number of different types of local government in Great Britain. The two main types are county boroughs, which are the bigger chartered towns, usually with a population in excess of 75,000, and administrative counties. The administrative

A less strenuous aspect of the Duke of Edinburgh's Award expedition section

Primary school children watching an educational television broadcast

counties in turn are subdivided into county districts (the smaller chartered towns); urban districts (towns without charters); and rural districts. Rural districts have even smaller subdivisions known as parishes. Each of these divisions has its own elected council.

Administrative counties Each of these is governed by an elected county council consisting of a chairman, aldermen and councillors. The chairman of the county council is elected annually by the council, which also appoints a vice chairman. Each councillor represents a district in the county and councillors are elected every three years.

The aldermen are elected for six years by the councillors. Half the number of aldermen retire every three years. As a rule the county council holds four meeting a year of the full council.

Urban and rural districts These consist of a chairman and councillors. The chairman is elected annually by the councillors. He may be a councillor or elected from outside the council. Elections for district councillors take place either annually or triennially, the councillors holding office for three years.

Parishes Rural parishes with a population of 300 or more are required to have a parish council. This consists of a chairman and not less than five and not more than twenty-one members (as determined by the county council). Members hold office for three years; one third of them are re-elected or replaced annually.

Boroughs A borough is created by Royal Charter. If the borough is a city the corporation consists of the mayor, aldermen and citizens. The mayor is usually elected from among the council.

Elections The same system of election applies to almost all local government councils. A person may be considered a local government elector if he or she lives in the council area or occupies as owner or tenant any rateable land or premises in the area with a yearly value of not less than £10.

Candidates for election as councillors must be of British nationality and must either be registered as an elector in the area in question, or have lived in that area for 12 months before the election or own land in the area. Members of the council cannot be elected from among employees of the council. Certain people are barred from standing for election; these include undischarged bankrupts and persons convicted of illegal or corrupt election practices.

Most candidates stand as representatives of one of the national political parties but some stand as independents. Each candidate must be nominated by two electors as proposer and seconder.

Voting takes place by secret ballot at polling stations under the supervision of a presiding officer.

Employees of local councils Local councils administer a wide range of public services. These come under the following headings:
Protective services These are the fire service, civil defence service, police service.
Personal services These are primarily concerned with health and welfare, education and housing.
Environmental services These are designed to secure local good order, amenities and public health. They include the inspection and abatement of nuisances, drainage, sewerage, street cleansing, refuse collection and disposal, rodent control etc.

When the children have been given a chance to assimilate the information given above they should be ready to make their trip and then get on with their follow up activities.

References

1   H. C. Barnard *An Introduction to Teaching* ULP 1965 second edition

6

Natural history, pets, gardens

The main out of school activities connected with natural history are usually nature rambles and building and maintaining homes and adequate living conditions for pets and other creatures under observation. Some schools with enough ground to spare will also have gardens and the supervision of these will often be the responsibility of a member of the staff. The books listed at the end of this chapter are recommended for background information.

Nature walks and rambles
Before organizing any nature expeditions, the teacher should make sure that all the children have been thoroughly grounded in the behaviour that will be expected of them during the trip. Their main concern should be to avoid damaging the land they walk over and harming its occupants. Gates should be shut behind them, fields with growing crops skirted, all litter collected, and birds and animals left alone.

Although nature walks are normally associated with older children they can be used to good advantage with children of all ages. In *Nature Study for Infants* Janet Hastie writes:

> Nature lessons in the classroom have only a part to play. Nature study should be part of the children's daily lives. Journeys to and from school, nature walks, poems, stories and hymns should all provide opportunities to talk about and enjoy things of nature.[1]

Writing in the Froebel pamphlet *Activity and Experience in the Infant School* E. H. Waters confirms this view:

> A teacher observing her class . . . will realize frequently their recent experience finds expression in their play and serves as inspiration for creative effort. This means that part of her job is to provide opportunities for experience which will provide fresh materials for thought and action, especially when interest may seem to be flagging . . . This may often be gained outside the classroom and an observant teacher can make good use of very ordinary happenings. Perhaps coal is being unloaded in the school

playground and little children can be taken out to watch, to look at the big horses or the lorry and the coalmen with their black sacks, and possibly they may learn something of cellars and furnaces. Occasional walks may take them to see the trains and signals at a level crossing, or to shuffle through autumn leaves in the park, to see ducks on a pond or the big bus station, or to watch and hear the church bells being rung for practice. More ambitious visits may take them to the zoo or the river or a farm; invariably the new experience will be a source of new ideas which sooner or later will find expression in many different ways.[2]

No matter what the age of the children taking part, a nature walk will be of greatly increased value if it is planned beforehand and a definite objective or set of objectives aimed at. The first two or three rambles may be more general while the children are getting accustomed to the lie of the land, but once they know their way around each ramble should have a set purpose. It may be to observe birds or collect moths and butterflies, or any one of a dozen objectives. Examples of some of the more common activities are given below.

Bird watching This is not an activity to be shared by a large number of children as birds are shy and wary creatures, but for those children with patience and initiative bird watching can be a fascinating hobby.

The first thing to do is to get a good idea of where and when birds congregate in the area of the school. In an urban area with no parks or open spaces the birds will have to be attracted to the playground with caches of food and water. A bird table can be constructed – any flat surface will do. The children in the club should be encouraged to keep notebooks in which they jot down details of any new birds they see. The notes should be in the form of headings – size and markings, shape of feet and bill, flight and walk, song, other observations. The date on which each bird is seen should also be entered. When all these observations have been made they can be checked against an illustrated book of birds. *The Birds of the British Isles and their Eggs* by T. A. Coward (Warne 1969) is one of the most comprehensive but smaller books like *A Pocket Guide to British Birds* by R. S. R. Fitter and R. A. Richardson (Collins 1966 new edition) will do very well.

For those children who live close enough to the open country or woods to make a nature walk possible, more ambitious plans may be made. The children should be taught to move quietly in small groups, wearing subdued clothing in which browns and greens predominate. Older boys and girls can construct a hide from which to watch birds and make notes. This consists merely of a portable camouflaged box. It should be about 1½ m high and not more than 1 m square. Four light uprights should be strutted together. Two sides should be covered with suitably camouflaged groundsheets and the third side, from which the observations are to be made, of dark brown sacking with squares cut out for observing the birds. The fourth side may be left open for entry and exit. The hide should be covered with leaves and branches. Some naturalists advocate situating the hide in the appropriate spot and leaving it, while others suggest that it be left about a hundred metres away from the chosen area and then edged forward gradually.

Collecting butterflies and moths
In order to collect butterflies and moths successfully the children will need a good net mounted on a light cane. The net should be about 254–304 mm in diameter and the cane ought to be about 1½ m long. Each group should have more than one net as they are liable to tear and become useless. Other necessary equipment includes tweezers, a killing bottle and a relaxing box.

The tweezers are needed for handling the butterflies and moths. The killing bottle need only be an ordinary jam jar with some finely chopped laurel leaves placed on the bottom and covered with a double layer of gauze. These laurel leaves are poisonous to insects and any butterfly or moth placed in the killing jar will be overcome by their fumes. When the insect is dead it should be put in the relaxing box so that the body remains pliable. The relaxing box is a small tin box with a layer of damp cork in the bottom onto which the dead specimen should be pinned.

Back at school the children should start the process of mounting the butterfly. For this they will need setting boards and setting needles, pins and tracing cloth. A setting board is a flat piece of wood with a channel hollowed out down the middle. Different sizes of boards should be constructed for different sizes of insects. The butterfly should be removed from the relaxing box and its body placed in the groove of the setting board with the wings outspread. A setting needle – an ordinary needle with a cork pushed over the eye to make for easier handling – should be used to adjust the wings.

When the wings have been adjusted a narrow strip of tracing cloth, shiny side downwards, should be pinned to the board in front of one wing, stretched over the wing and the other end pinned just behind it. The same should be done with the other wing. The wings should then be adjusted again if necessary with the setting needle and broad strips of cloth pinned over the wings to cover them.

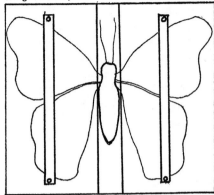

wings held in place

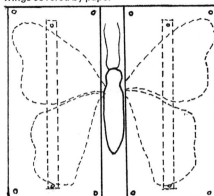

wings covered by paper

The setting boards and the attached moths and butterflies should then be placed somewhere safe, dry and warm and left for two to four weeks. At the end of that time they may be removed from the setting board and put on display in a cabinet or drawer.

Some natural history societies prefer to rear moths and butterflies rather than collect dead specimens. In order to do this the teacher and children should first construct an appropriate cage. One that can be used for many different kinds of insects is made in the following way:

1 Hinge together four glass plates of identical size with clear adhesive tape running the length of the glass.

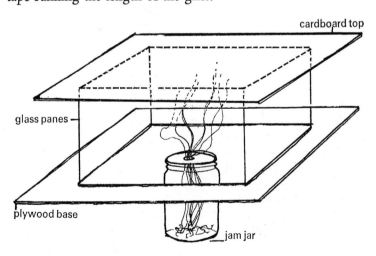

cardboard top

glass panes —

plywood base

jam jar

An insect cage

2 Cut two pieces of plywood for the base, one with the same measurements as the bottom of the glass cage, the other 12 mm larger.

3 Bore holes through the centre of each piece of plywood and stick them together to form a base with a larger rim running round it.

4 Slot the four hinged pieces of glass over the smaller board so that they rest on the larger one.

5 Place a piece of cardboard riddled with holes over the top to form a roof. The cage should then be balanced on top of a jam jar containing water and some kind of plant. The plant, which will be kept alive by the water in the jar, should be trained to grow through the hole in the floor of the cage.

When the caterpillars have been caught they can be deposited on the plant. The cage must be brushed out every two days and the plant changed for a fresh one regularly.

Ants

The best way to study ants is to keep a colony in the classroom in a formicarium. This too can be easily constructed.

1 Insert two sheets of window glass 254–304 mm square into a wooden frame with about 12 mm between each pane.

2 Attach a heavy base to the foot of the frame so that it stands upright like a window.

3 Cut a slot into the top of the frame and plug it with a piece of wood.

4 Drill a hole into one of the uprights about 25–50 mm from the top.

A formicarium

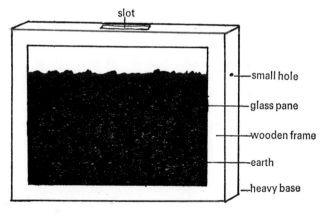

Construct two shutters of cardboard or similar material to fit into the frame over the glass on either side. These can be kept in place by slots fitted into the bottom of the frame. Ants will not work in the light and these shutters should only be removed for short periods for observation purposes.

When the formicarium has been constructed the plug in the top should be taken out and soil poured in up to the level of the hole 25 or 50 millimetres from the top.

Ants may be collected for the colony when an ant hill has been discovered. Part of the ant hill should be dug up and placed on a white cloth. As the ants scurry about they should be directed towards a clean bottle with the cork removed. Six or seven ants will enter the bottle at a time and by the time some ten bottles have been filled enough will have been gathered for the classroom. It is essential to capture the queen ant and as the queen is much larger than the others and there are sometimes six or seven to a colony this should not be too difficult. The ant hill should be shovelled back into place where the remaining ants will start to repair the damage.

The captured ants can be transferred to their new home through a paper funnel pushed into the slot in the frame. A little honey smeared inside the glass will do much to reconcile the ants to their new home.

Other collections

There are many ways of bringing nature into the classroom. Vivaria and aquaria may be constructed, pets such as tortoises, rabbits and hedgehogs kept and so on. *Exploration in the Junior School* by H. Philips and F. J. C. McInnes (ULP 1968) describes many ways in which children's love of animals may be turned to good account.

School gardens

Even in an urban school a spare patch of earth can sometimes be made into a school garden in order to add point and relevance to nature lessons. Not only can the children get to know flowers and shrubs but they will also meet, perhaps for the first time, such scourges as greenfly and other pests. No matter how small the garden the children should at least be able to produce enough to help feed the pets kept in the classroom. As long as they are given basic instruction in the use of spades, rakes and hoes and are given guidance in when and when not to plant seeds the children will find themselves with a fresh and rewarding interest.

References

1 Janet Hastie *Nature Study for Infants* Nelson 1960
2 E. H. Waters writing in *Activity and Experience in the Infant School* National Froebel Foundation 1960 fourth edition

Further reading

G. D. Fisher and J. Smyth *The Teacher's Book of Nature Study* Chambers 1964 fourth impression

H. Philips and F. McInnes *Exploration in the Junior School* ULP 1963 fifth impression

J. P. Volraith *Animals in Schools* UFAW 1956

J. O. Spoczynska *Inexpensive Pets* Wheaton 1965

R. W. Clark *Instructions to Young Ramblers* Museum Press 1958

S. R. Badmin *Trees in Britain* Penguin 1946

V. B. A. Gregory *Keeping of Animals and Plants in School* School Natural Science Society 1968 sixth edition

7

Clubs and youth organizations

There are many clubs and organizations which flourish as out of school activities. Some of these clubs are affiliated to national organizations, others are peculiar to an individual school. As far as the national organizations are concerned, further details may be obtained from their respective headquarters.

Boys' Brigade
Headquarters: Brigade House, Parsons Green, London sw6 The Boys' Brigade was founded in 1883. Its object is 'the advancement of Christ's Kingdom among boys and the promotion of habits of obedience, reverence, discipline, selfrespect, and all that tends towards a true Christian manliness'.

The Brigade is composed of companies of boys between 12 and 18 with an average strength of 40 members. Every company is attached to a church or some other Christian organization which means that a company cannot be started at a school unless arrangements are made to attach it to a church. The company officers and junior leaders are all voluntary workers nominated by the church. The company is divided into squads with senior boys as noncommissioned officers who in this way receive an early training in leadership and responsibility. The junior training reserve of the brigade, the Junior Boys' Brigade, is composed of boys between 9 and 12. Boys' Brigade companies are almost self supporting financially and the cost of national administration is largely borne by the companies and their friends.

Activities include Bible classes, regular attendance at church leading to communicant membership, church parades and a short service at every drill parade; classes in arts and craft, music, citizenship, first aid, life saving, fire fighting, signalling, map reading, nature study, seamanship and various forms of community service; physical training, athletics, gymnastics, indoor and outdoor games, swimming and camping.

The Scout Association
Headquarters: 25 Buckingham Palace Road, London sw1. The Associ-

ation was founded in 1908 by the late Lord Baden-Powell. Its aim is 'to provide opportunities for developing those qualities which make the good citizen – a man of honour, self disciplined and self reliant, willing and able to serve the community'.

The Association is international, interdenominational and non political. It has four main sections: Cub Scouts, aged 8 to 10; Scouts, aged 11 to 15; Venture Scouts, aged 16 to 20. There are also Sea Scouts and Air Scouts and a section for handicapped boys. The patrol system is a distinctive feature of the movement, encouraging both team spirit and training for leadership. Leadership training courses for the higher age groups and for adult members (Scouters) are an important activity.

The foundation of training is the Scout Promise and Law, voluntarily accepted by the boys on investiture. The ten laws each embody a positive ideal of conduct. Through the daily 'good turn' the Scout learns to help others. Camping is the basic activity and develops self reliance, initiative and resourcefulness. All the interests of outdoor life are encouraged. The badge system with its progressive tests encourages boys to be adaptable and observant and to find interesting and valuable hobbies.

The British Red Cross Society (Junior Branch)
Headquarters: 14 Grosvenor Crescent, London SW1
The junior branch of the Red Cross is an integral part of the British Red Cross Society which is nonpolitical, nonsectarian and has a threefold aim: 'the improvement of health, the prevention of disease and the mitigation of suffering.' The aim of the junior branch is to 'encourage young people to grow up in the tradition of voluntary service to the sick and suffering'.

The Junior Red Cross is organized in school groups known as links and in cadet units. Candidates are enrolled as members after attending at least six meetings of a cadet unit or link and passing a pre-enrolment test. To become a trained member of the Junior Red Cross a member must have passed Part I of the junior first aid or home nursing examination.

Training in first aid, nursing and kindred subjects, for which certificates are awarded, is adapted to the particular needs of young people so that as well as imparting technical knowledge, it encourages the members to give useful service in hospitals, children's homes and nurseries and in old people's homes and clubs. Such service will include making swabs, running errands, serving meals, arranging flowers and wheeling disabled patients in hospitals. Similar services are performed for sick and lonely old people in their own homes and for spastic and blind children. Many cadet units are proficient in the deaf/blind language. Camps for physically handicapped children are organized by the Junior Red Cross and summer camps are held for the members themselves.

Girl Guides Association
Headquarters: 17–19 Buckingham Palace Road, London SW1
The aim of the Association, which was founded by Lord Baden-Powell in 1910, is to provide a programme which promotes good citizenship by means of individual character training obtained through healthy and adventurous activities.

The Association is international without discrimination of race or religion. It is divided into three branches: Brownie Guides, aged 7 to 11; Guides, aged 10 to 16; Ranger Guides, aged 14 to 20. There is also the Extension Group for the handicapped. The patrol system is the basis of group planning. In Brownie Packs they work together to make decisions, in Guide companies they follow the patrol system and Ranger Guides elect their own Unit Council. There is a progressive degree of self programming so that under the Eight Point programme the girls may develop mental and physical qualities, character, creative ability, relationships with others, service, homecraft skills and enjoyment of the outdoors. Leadership training courses for Guiders and adult members are held at training centres.

Guiding aims to challenge a girl to participate fully in activities from each of the eight points. Yearly eight point badges are awarded for all round progress and service badges encourage girls to specialize in subjects which particularly interest them. The Guide Promise and the ten Guide Laws embody a practical code of ethics and every encouragement is given to girls to become active members of their own faith.

Girls' Brigade
Headquarters: Brigade House, 8 Parsons Green, London SW6
The aim of the Brigade which was founded in 1902 is 'to help girls to become followers of the Lord Jesus Christ, and through reverence, self control and a sense of responsibility to find true enrichment of life'.

The movement is interdenominational and international. The Brigade is composed of companies, each of which is connected with a church mission or other Christian organization, which must be remembered should a teacher want to start a company. Each company is graded into four sections according to age: Explorers, aged 5 to 8; Juniors, aged 8 to 11; Seniors, aged 11 to 14; Brigaders, aged 14 and over. All members wear uniform and must be total abstainers from intoxicating liquor and must attend Sunday school or company Bible class until they are 15; thereafter regular attendance at school is expected.

Training is given in citizenship, household management, child welfare, first aid, home nursing and personal hygiene, life saving and drill, as well as in arts, crafts and hobbies. Badges are awarded for proficiency in these and similar subjects. Opportunities for camping, swimming, rambling and cycling are arranged at country houses belonging to the Brigade.

National Association of Boys' Clubs
Headquarters: 17 Bedford Square, London WC1
The aim of the association is 'the promotion of the mental, physical and spiritual well being of boys, by the establishment and development of boys' clubs throughout the United Kingdom'. The Association is concerned primarily with the 14 to 18 age group.

Activities vary greatly according to the number of members, the nature of the premises and equipment, and the number of nights on which the club meets. The clubs try to give boys the opportunity to become physically fit and also to develop an interest in drama, handicrafts, music and other cultural subjects. Boys are given a share in management and responsibility, are helped to develop self discipline and given an opportunity to learn sufficient of the Christian faith to make up their own minds about accepting its challenge.

National Association of Youth Clubs
Headquarters: 30 Devonshire Street, London WIN 2AP
The association aims 'to help boys and girls, through leisure time activities, so to develop their physical, mental and spiritual capacities that they may grow to maturity as individuals and as members of society'.

Most of the members are between the ages of 14 and 20. The National Association acts as a coordinating and promoting body throughout the United Kingdom.

Physical activity both indoors and out of doors is encouraged, discussion and study groups, religious services and talks are arranged. Attention is given to the arts, especially music, drama, crafts and design, and to practical subjects such as cookery, carpentry, home nursing and health education.

National Federation of Young Farmers' Clubs
Headquarters: 55 Gower Street, London WC1
The principal objects are to form clubs to develop the individual

capacity of young people and their ability to serve the community; to encourage a greater sense of the importance of the agricultural industry and an appreciation of country life; to train young people in the arts of citizenship and in the science of farming.

Membership is open to young people between 10 and 25 years of age. Clubs are encouraged to form junior and senior sections and to plan variations in their programmes to suit particular age groups. Each club is a self governing body and has the support of an adult advisory committee which is elected by the club and on which local farmers are represented.

Club programmes include educational, recreational and social activities. The winter programme consists mainly of lectures; in the summer there are visits to farms, educational institutes, other clubs and other counties. Group work is a feature in many clubs and instruction is given in agricultural subjects and in rural and home crafts. A scheme of national proficiency tests in farm and farmhouse crafts has been instituted.

The St John Ambulance Brigade Cadets
Headquarters: 8 Grosvenor Crescent, London SW1
The Brigade is not denominational but as a descendant of the religious order of St John of Jerusalem, its training is based on spiritual ideals. The aims of the movement are to instruct members in first aid, home nursing and kindred subjects and to prepare them for entry into the adult divisions of the Brigade; to train for citizenship by working and playing together as a team; to improve health by special training and physical recreation.

Membership is open to boys and girls between the ages of 11 and 15, with special sections for students between the ages of 16 and 20, and juniors between the ages of 8 and 11. Cadets before enrolling must gain a first aid certificate and nursing (girl) cadets are subsequently required to qualify for a home nursing certificate.

Besides first aid and home nursing, other subjects which may be studied include citizenship, hygiene, child welfare, history of the Order, cooking, handicrafts, housecraft, fire fighting, swimming and life saving. Cadets may undertake duties in hospitals or in day or residential nurseries.

Youth Hostels Association
Headquarters: Trevelyan House, St Albans, Hertfordshire
The Youth Hostels Association was founded in 1930 to help young people, especially those of limited means, to a greater knowledge and

love of the countryside, by providing hostels or other simple accommodation for them throughout the country.

Membership is open to all persons over the age of 5 resident in England and Wales – separate but similar organizations exist in Scotland and Northern Ireland. Members are entitled to use the many hostels in the United Kingdom and throughout the world.

Members' knowledge of the countryside is increased through countryside discovery courses, held with the cooperation of the National Parks Commission and other bodies and by adventure holidays designed to give participants country holidays combined with some activity, such as sailing, pony trekking or sketching.

Combined Cadet Force
Headquarters: 58 Buckingham Gate, London sw1
The aim of the ccf is to provide boys with the framework of a disciplined organization within which qualities of endurance, resourcefulness and responsibility, together with a background knowledge of Service methods and conditions may be developed.

The Outward Bound Trust
Headquarters: Iddesleigh House, Caxton Street, London sw1
This was established in 1946 and is based on the theories of Kurt Hahn who believed that every boy should be given experience of adventure early in life to enable him to gain insight into his own character.

A sea school at Aberdovey in north Wales has been joined by other sea and mountain schools throughout Great Britain. A school specifically for girls has been opened at Towyn, near Aberdovey.

Industrial companies, education authorities, police forces, stores and banks as well as various public voluntary organizations, sponsor their boys and girls for outward bound training. Each of the boys' courses, catering for about 100 boys at a time, lasts one month and after fitness and skill have been acquired in preliminary training, major efforts are undertaken on sea or land.

The Duke of Edinburgh's Award
Headquarters: 2 Old Queen Street, London sw1
The various schemes of the Award, mainly for boys and girls between the ages 14 and 20, were designed 'to help both the young and those who take an interest in their welfare . . . . as an introduction to leisure time activities, a challenge to the individual to personal achievement'.

Boys are required to undertake four different activities: a service section of training in first aid in order to help others; a hobby of the boy's choice pursued for at least six months; one of a variety of physical fitness tests; an expedition undertaken in a group. The four activities for girls are 'design for living' which includes grooming and poise, setting up and running a home; interests, such as arts, crafts or physical activities pursued for at least six months; adventure, entailing planning and carrying out an enterprise away from home, and in the senior tests attending a residential training course; service, including first aid, home safety, mothercraft. In each category there are three standards of achievement, known as the bronze, silver and gold awards, designed for different age groups (boys 14 to 16, 15 to 18 and 16 to 19; and girls 14 to 17, 15 to 19 and 16 to 20).

Schoolclubs and societies
In addition to the national organizations which sometimes run clubs as out of school activities, there are many private clubs which enthusiastic teachers can organize and supervise after school hours. Social clubs with dances are always popular; all games both indoor and outdoor have their following and the different arts and crafts all attract children. In order to obtain basic information about some pastimes which could give rise to a school society teachers might find the following books useful.
D. A. Evans *12 Dramatic Interludes for Tape Recording* Wheaton 1968
N. J. Atkinson *Modern Teaching Aids* Maclaren 1966
V. Bruce *Dance and Drama in Education* Pergamon Press 1968
Bill and Sue Severn *Let's Give a Show* Kaye and Ward 1960
C. Cowell *Your Gardening Book* Faber 1954
J. C. Gagg *Gardens and Gardening* Blackwell 1961
I have included a brief account of some other clubs and societies which are normally popular with children.

Archaeological societies
A number of schools have local history societies, fewer possess archaelogical societies. Yet if the teacher in charge is enthusiastic and the area is one with an interesting history, a school society can flourish. The first thing that the teacher in charge should do is to contact the secretary of the local archaeological society if there is one and ask him if a member of the society could come along to the school to talk to the pupils and if possible bring with him examples gleaned from local digs. In the same way the curator of the local museum could be asked if he too would give an illustrated talk.

Once contact has been made with the local archaeological society, the teacher should try to make the most of this contact. Perhaps the children will be allowed to go and watch the members of the society at a dig one weekend. Later the children may be allowed to take part themselves, but they should only do so with permission and under supervision. As John Chambers points out in an article in *Teachers World*:

Teachers who set up archaeological societies will find that the members are raring to get out and dig. But the children will have to be restrained. Archaeological excavation is a highly skilled procedure and great and irreparable damage can be done by enthusiastic but ignorant amateurs.[1]

Even so, children can make archaeological finds without digging into the bowels of the earth. If they keep their eyes open they may find bone and flint artifacts, pieces of pottery etc in quarries, valleys, even in open fields.

The school society should meet regularly and with the aid of outside experts try to identify everything its members find and then relate the discoveries to events and periods in local and national history. Displays and exhibitions can be arranged for the benefit of the rest of the school and a society diary should be kept in which a record of all discoveries may be entered.

Discussion and debating societies

Debating societies are popular with many children, although some of them have to be coaxed into speaking in the earlier stages. Much depends upon the ability and personality of the chairman, usually the the teacher, as to whether the society is a success or not.

Children find in the society an opportunity to clarify their ideas, let off steam and make contact with fresh thoughts and other points of view. After a while the members will often come up with their own subjects for debate but in the initial stages the teacher will usually have to do this. When selecting a topic, which should of course be relevant and of interest to the children, it does no harm to make it mildly controversial and it helps if it is the sort of problem which cannot be answered by an outright yes or no. At the end of each debate those engaged in it should be asked for suggestions for the next debate.

In the earlier stages in order to stimulate interest and build up confidence the debates could be held in a number of forms – quizzes, parliamentary debates, forums etc. The leader should not play too obtrusive a part but see to it that all aspects of the question under review are brought out and that everyone has a chance to speak.

Later more formal debates should be held with proposer and seconder, opposer and seconder, recorder and so on. The chairman should sum up the debate and help the children see where they have gone wrong.

Film society

A film society can have two functions – it can introduce children to a planned programme of films and increase their knowledge of film both as an art and as an entertainment medium and it can also, in a few schools, enable the children to make their own films.

Any teacher who needs help in compiling a list of films to show to the children in the school club is recommended to read the various publications of the Society for Education in Film and Television, particularly the annual *Screen Education Yearbook* which contains many articles of interest, lists of societies and organizations providing films etc.

A course should be chosen primarily for entertainment value but should also include, if possible, examples of the development of film as an art form, films which will extend the range and experience of the audience and films which will stimulate the children to discussion and other follow up activities.

Teachers who are thinking of allowing the school society to make a film should read *Young Film Makers Symposium* editor H. R. Wills (SEFT Publications 1964). Another useful book from SEFT Publications is *Young Film Makers* by S. Rees and D. Waters (1963). The *Amateur Movie Maker* magazine may also be of assistance.

Expense will be the major drawback when making a film. Some equipment may be borrowed but, as is more likely, if the society has to buy all its own equipment the costs will mount up. For further details the teacher is recommended to read a most comprehensive book on the subject *How to Make Films at School* J. D. Beal (Focal Press 1968).

If hiring films, these firms will supply comprehensive catalogues at very small cost (others are listed in *Screen Education Year Book*):
Columbia Picture Corporation, 16 mm Division, 142 Wardour Street, London WIV 4AH
Connoisseur Films, 58 Wardour Street, London WIV 4DS
Gala Film Distributors, 13/17 Old Compton Street, London WIV 6JR
Rank Film Library, 1 Aintree Road, Perivale, Middlesex

Many firms and organizations issue publicity films free of charge. For a list of these organizations see the *Treasure Chest for Teachers* (Schoolmaster 1965 revised edition).

Music societies

As a general rule music is a subject for the enthusiast if not the specialist and it would not, for example, be much use for a tone deaf teacher, no matter how enthusiastic, to form a school music society. For someone interested in music a great deal of enjoyment can be derived from helping with a school choir or orchestra. For those teachers willing to attempt to found such a society but not too sure of their ground, the following books are recommended:

J. B. Dalby *School and Amateur Orchestras* Pergamon Press 1968
E. Priestley, F. Fowler, C. Dolmetsch *The School Recorder Books* Arnold 1968
G. Winters *An Introduction to Group Music Making* Chappel 1967

Philatelic societies
A large number of children enjoy collecting stamps and a school society will enable them to meet other children of similar interests, learn more about stamps and how to collect them, and arrange swaps and purchases.

Apart from being an interesting and educative hobby stamp collecting can also be lucrative. The British Guiana one cent 1856 stamp for which thousands of pounds changed hands once belonged to a schoolboy who found it on an envelope in an attic. The boy sold the stamp for six shillings, which might be used as a moral tale when children are told to study the stamps in their collection but not to expect to make a fortune from their sale!

In addition to providing a room in which the children can meet after school to compare stamps, the teacher can also help by providing a certain amount of basic equipment. A good catalogue (preferably Stanley Gibbons) should be available and the children should be shown the right way to use tweezers for handling stamps, stock books for carrying spare stamps, perforation gauges, watermark detectors and so on.

References
1 John Chambers writing in *Teachers World* 5th April 1968

8

Other activities

Most of the activities mentioned so far have been those designed to take place out of the classroom as part of the extracurricular life of the school. There are also some spare time activities which will enable the teacher to improve and extend the range of his or her classroom teaching and these activities will be discussed in this chapter.

Foremost among these activities comes the construction and maintenance of audio-visual aids, in particular mechanical teaching aids such as radio, television sets, tape recorders, film and filmstrip projectors and overhead projectors. Although these aids will be used almost exclusively in the classroom the teacher will have to manufacture them or learn how to operate them largely as an out of school activity.

A number of books will prove useful in this context. They include:
G. Kent *Blackboard to Computer* Ward Lock Educational 1969
N. J. Atkinson *Modern Teaching Aids* Maclaren 1966
R. Cable *Audio-Visual Handbook* ULP 1965

Radio sets

The Schools Broadcasting Department of the BBC provides a wide range of radio programmes for all ages which cover most of the subjects on the school timetable. Any teacher wishing for details in advance should see the material sent round to the schools by the Schools Broadcasting Council and then buy the appropriate notes for the teacher and pupils' pamphlets.

To receive programmes in the classroom the teacher will need either an ordinary radio set in the classroom or the school may possess a central receiver, probably situated in the headteacher's study, with loudspeaker extensions in the classroom.

The type of radio set used is immaterial provided reception is clear. Usually there is no need for an aerial but in remote areas reception may be improved if one is used. Constructing a simple aerial poses few problems. On the radio set there will be two sockets, one marked A (for aerial) and one marked E (for earth). The aerial can be a length of bare wire as long and as high as possible, suspended between two supports outside the school. The wire collects the radio waves and the important thing is that they should then be taken to the radio set without touching anything. This means that the aerial wire must be insulated from its support at either end by being suspended between pieces of rope. The horizontal aerial wire should then be connected to the set by a piece of insulated wire as shown in the diagram.

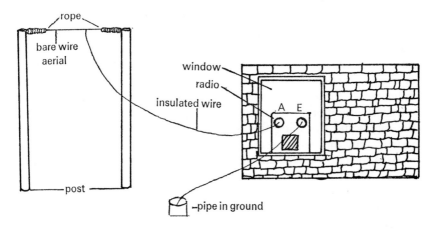

Another wire runs from the earth socket on the radio set into the ground – connecting the metal wire to a piece of iron pipe dug into the ground is a good idea.

This aerial and earth installation should, for safety's sake, be checked by a qualified electrician. On no account should children be allowed to have anything to do with it.

Most schools prefer to have one central receiver with loudspeaker extensions to the classrooms because this simple and sturdy classroom system cannot be upset or damaged as easily as a radio set. Such a system should be installed by an electrician, not a member of the staff.

For advice on the general preparation for schools broadcasts teachers should read the relevant chapter in *Blackboard to Computer*.

Television sets

With the BBC and the independent television companies both putting out extensive educational services and the growth of closed circuit educational television in many areas most teachers are making some use of television in the classroom.

While television sets must be installed and serviced by professional engineers the teacher can still play his or her part in ensuring that the children obtain the maximum benefit from the school set. No child should be seated farther than 6 metres or closer than one and a half metres from the set. The viewing room need not be blacked out. The bottom of the set should be some 2 metres from the floor and the seats should be so arranged that no child has to watch at an angle of more than 45 degrees from the centre of the set.

Tape recorders

Tape recorders are now used for a variety of purposes in schools and operating these instruments is well within the capabilities of any teacher. Care should be taken that the microphone is correctly placed, preferably on a stand. The recorder may then be plugged in (if electrically operated) or the batteries checked if it is battery operated. After setting the speed indicator at the required speed ($3\frac{3}{4}$ ips is usually adequate for most purposes although for recording music $7\frac{1}{2}$ ips is even better) putting on the spools and threading the tape through as directed in the book of instructions, the machine may then be switched on, the appropriate control to start the tape and recording pressed and the recording will begin. When the recording is over, the machine should be stopped, and the tape rewound.

In order to listen to the tape the playback control should be used. Afterwards rewind the tape until it is all on one spool. The tape can then be taken off the machine and used again and again as each subsequent recording wipes off or obliterates the one before.

In order to tape record radio programmes the teacher should join the input socket of the tape recorder to the output socket on the radio marked *external loudspeaker*. If both radio and recorder are connected to the mains the recorder should be switched onto record and the radio adjusted to the correct wavelength and volume.

Film projectors

Film comes in three sizes – 8 mm, 16 mm, and 35 mm. The latter is the standard size for commercial films while 8 mm is the average home movie size. Most educational films are in 16 mm. Most teachers will find it useful to be able to operate a standard projector as films are now used both as a classroom aid and an end of term treat.

Projectors may vary from make to make and the teacher is advised to read the manual accompanying the particular one in his or her school but the basic sequence generally remains the same.

The screen and projector should be placed in position and seating for the children arranged in advance. The projector and any loudspeaker extensions should be plugged in, the windows blacked out and the electric light turned on. When this has been done the power supply on the projector may be turned on. The light on the machine should also be turned on and a square or rectangle of light should now be projected onto the screen.

At this point the teacher should pick up the film, having previously examined it to make sure that it is the correct one and that it is wound round the right way. It may now be inserted into the projector.

In order to do this the teacher should stand in front of the projector and face it. The film should be held up and unrolled until the title frame is visible. If the title frame can be read the right way round the film is being held in the correct position. Remembering to keep the film in this position the teacher may then walk back to the side of the projector and insert the film.

The film is then wound on. There may be some minor variations in the way this is done but generally the perforations on the side of the film are fed onto the sprockets on the projector and wound on using the inching mechanism on the side of the machine. To make sure that the film has been inserted correctly and to adjust the focus turn on the motor and make any adjustments. By now the film should be ready to be shown.

Filmstrip projectors

The most common projector is the ordinary 35 mm filmstrip and slide projector. Slides must be inserted and withdrawn singly but a filmstrip is of course joined together and must be wound onto the projector. The instruction manual will explain how to do this in detail. It should be remembered that the strip is fed into the projector upside down and it is turned the right way up by the lens when projected onto the screen.

Overhead projectors

The overhead projector is designed to throw an image over the shoulder or head of the person using it so that a picture appears on a screen behind him. The teacher merely writes or draws on a special pad on the projector and by pressing a button transfers the picture to the screen.

First aid

All teachers should have a basic knowledge of first aid and those who are going to spend a considerable amount of their spare time with children in a number of out of school activities must acquire a sound working knowledge. Needless to say no time should be lost in calling a doctor in the case of an accident which the teacher even suspects might be serious. The teacher should remember the definition of first aid given in the *First Aid Junior Manual* of the British Red Cross Society: 'It is the help given at once to injured people or to those suddenly taken ill before the expert (doctor or nurse) takes over or the ambulance arrives.'[1]

Bleeding, bruising and grazing are among the most common injuries suffered by children. In the case of slight bleeding the teacher should try to protect the wound by cleaning it with a swab. If the wound is very slight the blood may be washed away under a running tap. After the affected area has been gently cleaned, a piece of clean gauze may be placed over it and cotton wool and a bandage placed over the top.

If the bleeding is heavy the affected part should be raised and the teacher should grip it firmly to control the flow of blood. When this has been achieved a dressing should be placed over the wound and more dressings added if the blood still seeps through. This is strictly a temporary measure and expert aid should be sent for as soon as possible.

Grazes may be treated in the same way as minor bleeding i.e. the area cleaned with a swab and if necessary a dressing applied. Bruises can be treated with a cold compress (a handkerchief, towel etc) soaked, wrung out and applied to the bruise.

Shock may follow any accident. Any person suffering from shock should be made to lie down, a support should be placed under his head and blankets or overcoats put over him while an ambulance is sent for.

Sometimes a child may be burned by fire or electricity. If the teacher is on the spot cold water may be applied to the affected area. If the teacher arrives later the burnt area should not be washed but covered with a dry dressing and bandage until expert help arrives.

Any teacher should obtain a good first aid manual – those issued by the British Red Cross Society are excellent – and make sure that he or she has an outline knowledge of the subject in case of emergency.

Summary

Any teacher who undertakes out of school activities will find that his hours of work are extended, his responsibilities increased and, in all probability, his nervous system subjected to a number of shocks. At the same time he will enter into a new and closer relationship with the children he teaches, enrich the life of the school and often enjoy himself thoroughly in the process.

References

1 *First Aid Junior Manual* British Red Cross Society reprinted 1969

Bibliography

John Allen *Play Production* Dobson 1950
N. J. Atkinson *Modern Teaching Aids* Maclaren 1966
H. C. Barnard *An Introduction to Teaching* ULP 1965 second edition
J. D. Beal *How to Make Films at School* Focal Press 1968
Grace Brown *Mime in Schools and Clubs* Macdonald and Evans 1953
V. Bruce *Dance and Drama in Education* Pergamon Press 1968
R. Cable *Audio-Visual Handbook* ULP 1965
Careers Guide HMSO 1968
Marjorie Chambers *Introduction to Dewey Decimal Classification for British Schools* Gresswell 1961
R. W. Clark *Instructions to Young Ramblers* Museum Press 1958
J. B. Dalby *School and Amateur Orchestras* Pergamon Press 1968
Joseph Edmundson *PE Teachers' Handbook for Primary Schools* Evans 1956
First Aid Junior Manual British Red Cross Society 1969
G. D. Fisher and J. Smyth *The Teacher's Book of Nature Study* Chambers 1964 fourth impression
J. C. Gagg *Gardens and Gardening* Blackwell 1961
B. Heap *A Guide to Careers and Courses* Ward Lock Educational 1969
G. Kent *Blackboard to Computer* Ward Lock Educational 1969
Barbara Kyle *Teach Yourself Librarianship* EUP 1964
Middle School Choice Careers Research and Advisory Centre 1967
Elizabeth Morgan *A Practical Guide to Drama in the Primary School* Ward Lock Educational 1969
R. N. Pemberton-Billing and J. D. Clegg *Teaching Drama* ULP 1965
Planning the Programme HMSO 1953
Barbara Priestley *British Qualifications* Deutsch 1966
R. W. Purton *Surrounded by Books: The Library in the Primary School* Ward Lock Educational 1962
M. W. Randall and W. K. Waine *Objectives in Physical Education* Bell 1968

Report on Education No 54: The Public Library Service and You Department of Education and Science 1969

Julie M. Sharpe *PE Teachers' Handbook for Infant Schools* Evans 1959

J. O. Spoczynska *Inexpensive Pets* Wheaton 1965

Index